WORKING WITH INDIVIDUALIZED INSTRUCTION

"We are, I think,
in the right road
of improvement,
for we are mak-
ing experiments."
BENJAMIN FRANKLIN

WORKING WITH
INDIVIDUALIZED
INSTRUCTION

THE DULUTH EXPERIENCE

THORWALD ESBENSEN

Assistant Superintendent in Charge of
Instruction, Duluth Public Schools

85465

With a Foreword by **Robert F. Mager**

Fearon Publishers, Belmont, California

DEDICATED TO THE MEMORY OF MY FATHER,
GEORGE ESBENSEN

FOREWORD

Working with Individualized Instruction is the story of a school system that decided to give its students a better education, and then organized itself to do so without government funds, without the support or encouragement of a university department of education, without the financial or electro-mechanical support of industry, and without a small mountain of hardware. It is the story of a group of teachers who applied the seat of their pants to the seat of their chairs, who faced the uncertainty associated with doing things differently, and who began working harder than anyone had a right to expect. This book is about individualized instruction in action.

But just what *is* individualized instruction?

Though many pay lip service to an intent to design instruction to fit the needs of the individual student, much seems to be lost between the lip and the classroom. For this reason it might be well to review the essentials of individualized instruction so that you may determine for yourself whether the Duluth projects fulfill the requirements of a student-oriented system.

Individualized instruction is not the same thing as "teaching students individually." An instructional system is individualized when the characteristics of each student play a major part in the selection of objectives, materials, procedures, and time. It is individualized when *decisions* about objectives and how to achieve them are based on the individual student. One does not simply say that a system is or is not individualized, however, for it is not a black or white matter. Rather, one tries to identify the *nature* and *degree* of individualization.

The questions that follow can be asked of any instructional system to determine the degree to which it pays attention to the needs of the individual student. They may be asked of the projects described in this book. The answers expected of an instructional system that is highly attentive to the individual student are given after each question.

- Are the instructional objectives written on paper?   YES
- Are the content objectives given to the student?   YES
- Are all students expected to achieve the same objectives?   NO

- Do all students use the same instructional materials (e.g., texts)? _NO_
- Are all students expected to follow the same procedure while in the classroom? _NO_
- Do all students work at each subject for the same amount of time? _NO_
- Do students spend most of their classroom time doing that which everyone else is doing? _NO_

Who makes the decisions? Despite his imperfect self-knowledge, the student knows more about himself than we do. Therefore, if we are to come closest to selecting the most appropriate materials, procedures, time, and objectives, the student himself must do a large part of the selecting. The questions that follow bear on this aspect of the individualized instruction system. Again, the answers given indicate how well the instructional system is individualized.

- May the student have any part in deciding which objectives he will be expected to achieve? _YES_
- May the student decide which materials he will use in trying to achieve an objective? _YES_
- May the student decide which procedures he will follow in attempting to achieve an objective? _YES_
- May the student decide how much time he will devote to an activity? _YES_

One determines the degree of individualization, then, by asking *which* instructional decisions have been made and *by whom* they were made. In a highly individualized system, the teacher, the school, and the community make most of the decisions about *what* the student is expected to achieve, and the student makes most of the decisions about *how* he will achieve.

I think you will see that this is just about how things have been done and are being done in Duluth's project schools. The educators who are working in those project schools have not solved all of the problems of education, nor do they claim to have done so. But they have moved a giant step in that direction. The winds of change are blowing over American education, and the Duluth Public Schools system is one of the huffers and puffers.

ROBERT F. MAGER

Preface

"It is my prediction," says R. Louis Bright, Associate Commissioner for Research, United States Office of Education, "that within another ten years almost the entire academic portion of instruction will be on an individual basis in most schools." *Working with Individualized Instruction* is an attempt to describe how one school system of approximately 22,000 students is moving in this direction.

In offering this recounting of the Duluth experience, attention has been paid primarily to three elementary school projects with widely varying student populations. It should be pointed out, however, that other schools within the system (including those serving junior and senior high school students) are also involved in projects of considerable significance, and all of these efforts add up to a concerted push in the direction of Mr. Bright's forecast.

It is my hope that teachers and administrators alike will find the Duluth venture relevant to their own circumstances. There would be little point in describing a program whose viability depended on special conditions that could not be duplicated elsewhere. The fact is, Duluth's individualized programs are being conducted in a wide variety of school settings, and our first project was supported entirely from within our own operating budget.

I owe many thanks to my secretary, Mrs. Vivian Logan, and to Sister Margaret James, of the College of St. Scholastica, for their help in the preparation of the original manuscript.

THORWALD ESBENSEN

CONTENTS

1234

Individualized Instruction

Individualized instruction has long been a goal of American education. Ideally, individualized instruction means an arrangement that makes it possible at all times for each student to be engaged in learning those things that are most appropriate for himself as an individual. This ideal can never be reached, of course. The best we can do is move toward it. The purpose of this book is to suggest how this might be done.

Let's begin by clearing up some misconceptions. Individualized instruction is not the same as independent study. To be sure, independent study is often a part of individualized instruction. But individualized instruction is the larger idea. It includes inde-

1

pendent study as one way of doing things. Failure to make this distinction may be the reason why some educators assert that individualized instruction cannot be expected to work out well at the kindergarten-primary level.

Individualized instruction is not tied to team teaching or flexible scheduling. Although new staffing patterns and ways of dividing the school day are frequently associated with the decision to individualize instruction, such changes are not always essential. Under certain circumstances, a self-contained classroom might be just what is needed.

To put the matter in general terms, individualized instruction does not depend for its success upon any given arrangement of persons, materials, or environmental conditions. The formal structure that proves to be most effective in one instance may turn out to be inadequate in another. Each situation is in some respects unique, and should be treated accordingly. Having said this, however, we must also recognize that individualized instruction does not occur in a vacuum. Certain classroom settings and practices do look more promising than others. In this sense we can, without being dogmatic, recommend specific procedures that may be widely applicable.

Instituting an Individualized Instruction Program

The first piece of advice for your consideration when instituting a program of individualized instruction is to start small. There is nothing to the notion that you have to institute this kind of program "across the board." A single classroom with an imaginative teacher is all you need to begin. But then you must give special support. Here there must be no stinting.

In order to buy instructional materials and equipment above and beyond the items usually found in the traditional classroom, each teacher will need an initial budget of approximately two thousand dollars, plus another thousand for the second year. It is important that the teacher have wide latitude in securing materials. If he must prove in advance the effectiveness of everything he wants to purchase, he will tend to hedge his bets, and his enthusiasm will begin to wane.

All teachers in the individualized instruction program should be volunteers. There is no faster way to kill a program than to staff it with reluctant dragons. The unwilling teacher is the deadliest critic there is. To place the fate of an educational venture in unfriendly hands is to court disaster.

Selection of staff should be followed by in-service work designed to provide teachers with the know-how necessary to conduct a program of individualized instruction. Operationally, the central problem of individualized instruction is the problem of classroom management. Therefore, whatever else it may attempt to accomplish, a worthwhile in-service program will suggest how teachers may work effectively with students within a formal school environment.

Performance Objectives

Probably the best way to begin an individualized instruction program is by writing instructional objectives expressed in terms of observable student behavior. This is often a difficult thing for teachers to learn to do. The main reason for this would seem to be that in education the word "objective" has generally meant *purpose;* and when educators speak of purpose, they almost invariably use words such as "understanding," "comprehension," and "appreciation." These words point to noble aims; no question about that. But, *when left wholly in this form,* they do not refer to anything that is *directly observable* and, therefore, do not permit us to evaluate how well we are doing whatever it is we are trying to do.

The trick is to supplement each announcement of purpose with a statement of criterion performance. That is to say, each declaration of an instructional aim should be accompanied by a clear description of what the learner must be able to do in order to demonstrate his accomplishment of the objective.

The emphasis here is on the word "do," and the doing must be observable—a warm feeling in the pit of the stomach is not sufficient. For example, which of the following two statements is expressed in terms of observable student performance?

A. The student will have a good understanding of the letters of the alphabet, A through Z.

B. The student will be able to pronounce the names of the letters of the alphabet, A through Z.

Statement B tells what it is that the student will be able to *do*. He will be able to *pronounce* the names of the letters of the alphabet, A through Z. Statement A tells us that the student will have a good *understanding* of the letters of the alphabet. But this is not very clear. We cannot tell what it is that the student is supposed to be able to *do* as a result of this understanding.

Let's try another pair of statements. Which of these statements is expressed in terms of observable student performance?

A. The student will have an adequate comprehension of the mechanics of punctuation.

B. Given a sentence containing an error in punctuation, the student will correct the mistake.

Statement B tells what it is that the student will *do;* he will *correct* the error in punctuation. Statement A, which says that the student will have an adequate *comprehension* of the mechanics of punctuation, is rather cloudy. We cannot tell what it is that the student is supposed to be able to *do* as a result of his comprehension.

Mental Activity

At this point, an objection may be raised. Isn't the person who is *comprehending* something *doing* something? Isn't intellectual performance an acceptable kind of student performance? Certainly. The difficulty is that mental activity, *as such,* is not directly observable. We cannot literally open up a person's head and see the thinking that is going on inside. If it is to be of *use* to us, a statement of performance must *specify* some sort of behavior that *can be observed.*

This does not mean that we are not concerned about intellectual performance. It does mean that since mental activity, as such, is not directly observable, some sort of behavior that *is* observable will have to stand for, or represent, the intellectual performance we have in mind. For example, suppose we are interested in having students "know something about the writing style of Ernest Hemingway." Whatever may be intellectually involved in the attainment of this goal, it should be apparent that our aim, *as stated,* leaves much to be desired. What is the student who knows able to do that the student who does not know is not able to do? This is the important question, for we cannot measure the accomplishment of our instructional purpose until we have specified the relevant behavior. Although there is no single answer to the question we have posed (our objective of "knowing something" is too vague for that), here is a possible statement of desired performance:

> Given ten pairs of short prose passages—each pair having one selection by Ernest Hemingway and one by a different author— the student is able, with at least 90 per cent accuracy, to choose the ten selections written by Hemingway.

Conditions of Performance

A well-written statement of desired performance should not only say what it is that a student who has mastered the objective will be able to *do*, it should also say under what *conditions* the student will be able to do this.

Here is one of our earlier statements concerning the alphabet:

> The student will be able to pronounce the names of the letters of the alphabet, A through Z.

We have said that this statement is expressed in terms of student performance. Does this statement also set forth the conditions under which the performance is to take place? No, it does not. For one thing, we cannot tell from our statement whether the student is to pronounce the names of the letters at sight or from memory. If the letters are to be shown, we do not know whether the student is to work with capital letters, small letters, or both. Nor do we know whether the student is to work with these letters in regular sequence or in random order. Each set of conditions is substantially different from the rest, and will make its own special demands upon the student who attempts to accomplish the objective.

Let's examine two more statements. Which of these statements sets forth the *conditions* under which a certain kind of performance is to take place?

A. Given the Dolch list of the 95 most common nouns, the student will be able to pronounce correctly all the words on this list.

B. The student will be able to pronounce correctly at least 90 per cent of all words found in most beginning reading books.

Statement A, which tells us that the Dolch list of the 95 most common nouns will be used, sets the conditions for the demonstration of student mastery. We are told that these particular words, and no others, are the ones at issue for this objective. Statement B, offering us only the dubious clue of "words found in most beginning reading books," does not tell us enough. Our conditions need to be defined more precisely than this.

Level of Performance

We come now to the matter of performance *level*. A well-written statement of performance will establish, when appropriate, an acceptable minimum standard of achievement. Look at this statement:

> Given 20 sentences containing both common and proper nouns, the student will be able to identify, with very few mistakes, both kinds of nouns.

Does this statement establish a minimum standard of achievement? No, it does not. To say that the student is to perform "with very few mistakes" does not tell us enough. How many are "very few"? Here is the Hemingway example we looked at earlier:

> Given ten pairs of short prose passages—each pair having one selection by Ernest Hemingway and one by a different author— the student is able, with at least 90 per cent accuracy, to choose the ten selections written by Hemingway.

Does this establish a minimum standard of achievement? Yes, it does. The student is expected to be able, "with at least 90 per cent accuracy, to choose the ten selections written by Hemingway." This constitutes a minimum standard of achievement.

Let's try one more example:

> The student should be able to pronounce from memory, and in sequence, the names of the letters of the alphabet, A through Z.

Does this establish a minimum standard of achievement? Yes, it does. The statement implies that we are looking for 100 per cent mastery. However, we could, if we wanted to be explicit, restate the desired performance in this way:

The student should be able to pronounce from memory, in sequence, and with 100 per cent accuracy, the names of the letters of the alphabet, A through Z.

In a related manner, some learning tasks justifiably present the student with an all-or-nothing situation. For example, if the learner is supposed to be able to tie his shoe laces, it would not make sense to talk about his being able to do this with 90 per cent accuracy. Here the proposition is absolute: He either can tie his shoelaces or he cannot. There is nothing useful in between.

Instructional Materials for Objectives

An instructional objective should not ordinarily be limited to specific *means* (particular materials or methods), but should be stated in terms that permit the use of various procedures. Look at this statement of performance:

Given the California Test Bureau's E-F level programmed booklet on capitalization, the student is able to work through the exercises in this booklet with at least 90 per cent accuracy.

Is this statement limited to the use of a particular instructional item or procedure? Yes, it is. The desired performance is expressed exclusively in terms of work with a specific booklet. Although the particular kind of skill development that is promoted by this booklet is presumably also fostered by other instructional materials and methods, no such options are available under the terms of the statement of performance as it is now written.

Look at this statement of desired performance:

Given 20 sentences containing a variety of mistakes in capitalization, the student is able, with at least 90 per cent accuracy, to identify and rewrite correctly each word that has a mistake in capitalization.

Is this objective limited to the use of a particular instructional item or procedure? No, it is not. The desired performance, as now stated, permits the use of a number of instructional items that show promise in being able to help students attain the objective. These items might include not only the California Test Bureau's E-F level material, but also the somewhat simpler C-D level presentation, a programmed booklet by D. C. Heath,

Unit 11 of English 2200, Unit 9 of English 2600, Lessons 87 and 88 of English 3200, several filmstrips on capital letters, and so on.

Measuring Accomplishment

A well-written instructional objective will suggest how its accomplishment can be measured. This follows from our view that a well-written objective specifies under what *conditions* and, when appropriate, to what *extent* a certain kind of student *performance* can be expected to take place.

Look at this objective:

The student should know the alphabet.

Does this objective suggest how its accomplishment can be measured? No, it does not. The reason for this is that knowing the alphabet can mean different things to different people. Therefore, depending upon what is meant, the measuring of this knowing will take different forms.

Suppose we elaborate upon our objective so that it reads:

Shown the letters of the alphabet in random order (in both upper- and lower-case forms), the student is able to say the name of each letter with 100 per cent accuracy.

Does the objective now suggest how its accomplishment can be measured? Yes, it does. It tells us that the student will be shown the letters of the alphabet, that he will be shown these letters in both upper- and lower-case forms and in random order, and that he will be called upon to say with 100 per cent accuracy the name of each letter shown. The objective, in other words, makes plain how its accomplishment can be measured. If teachers at all levels of schooling would be this explicit in writing instructional objectives, they might reasonably hope to eliminate almost immediately one cause of learning failure among students: the traditional fuzziness of classroom assignments.

Format for Developing Objectives

Our in-service work in connection with individual instructional projects in the Duluth Public Schools has gradually led to the creation of a six-point format for developing instructional objectives, which follows.

Instructional Objective
1. Content classification.
2. Purpose.
3. Criterion performance.
4. Sample test situation.
5. Taxonomy category.
6. Resources.

We have already touched briefly on the matters of purpose, criterion performance, and sample test situation. Perhaps the best way of reviewing these elements, as well as explaining the remaining points listed above, is to construct an example that will illustrate in detail what we mean.

We shall choose an objective from the magic realm of creativity. There is a reason for doing this. Many people have the feeling that objectives expressed in terms of observable student behavior can be put together for some of the basic skills areas (map reading, spelling, etc.), but that nothing much can be done in this way when it comes to the humanities. If, therefore, our example can help to disprove this notion, we shall have served in double measure the cause of performance objectives.

The objective we have in mind has to do with the writing of haiku, Japanese poetry that contains three rhymeless lines of five, seven, and five syllables, respectively, for a total of seventeen syllables. Far from being an anemic academic exercise, the discipline of haiku somehow releases creative energies that are often imprisoned within the unlimited boundaries of student prose.

Let us turn to the task of setting forth our haiku objective under the headings of (1) content classification, (2) purpose, (3) criterion performance, (4) sample test situation, (5) taxonomy category, and (6) resources.

Content classification simply means the placement of an objective somewhere in a course or subject matter outline. In the present instance, we might treat this heading as follows:

Content Classification
I. Imaginative use of language.
   A. Poetry.
      1. Haiku.

The purpose of our objective:

Purpose

To engage students in a formal poetic exercise that will encourage brevity, relevance, and the use of words in fresh, new ways.

We have discussed criterion performance at length:

Criterion Performance

Given any item of experience (music, literature, film, an observed event, a recollection), the student will be able to make a personal response in the form of a haiku (seventeen syllables, 5-7-5, in three lines) of his own creation.

Next is the sample test situation. As our criterion performance makes plain, we have plenty of latitude here. One interesting possibility is to present the student with a literal English translation of some Japanese haiku and ask him to write his own haiku based upon whatever this translation suggests to him.

Sample Test Situation

Here is the literal English translation of a Japanese haiku: Caged-bird/butterflies envy/eye-expression. Look at the words carefully. Then write a haiku of your own, capturing whatever meaning the literal translation suggests to you.

If you are wondering just what a student might do with this problem, here is what one ninth grade girl came up with:

> The caged yellow bird
> envies the spring butterflies'
> remorseless freedom.

In keeping with our six-part format, we come now to the task of identifying the taxonomy category that most nearly fits our instructional objective. In developing this feature, we have been strongly influenced by Bloom.* The Bloom taxonomy uses six categories: knowledge, comprehension, application, analysis, synthesis, and evaluation. Although we have found Bloom's suggested heirarchy stimulating to explore and most helpful in making us keenly aware of a broad range of intellectual activi-

---

*Benjamin S. Bloom (ed.), *Taxonomy of Educational Objectives. Handbook I: Cognitive Domain.* New York: David McKay, Inc., 1956.

ties, we have gradually come around to working with a simpler taxonomy of our own construction.

Our classification scheme employs four categories: knowledge, comprehension, application, and invention. As is true of the Bloom taxonomy, our categories for classifying intellectual tasks are not as clear and distinct as one might wish. This is partly because cognitive accomplishments often include activities that are, in turn, appropriate to different categories. Perhaps the best way to resolve this difficulty is to focus upon the main thrust of an instructional objective and to classify it accordingly.

It should also be remembered that an intellectual task is frequently defined by the nature of the test items or situation used to measure its achievement. For example, if items identical to those the student has practiced on are used in the test situation, the subsequent feat of learning is probably one of simple recall or recognition.

Let us consider each of our four categories. The emphasis in our knowledge category is on simple recall and recognition—in other words, on memory. The student remembers specific items, such as names, statements, objects, procedures, etc. For example, the student who learns to arrange the letters of the alphabet in order from A to Z has acquired knowledge. That is to say, the order of the letters is arbitrary and, therefore, must be memorized. Similarly, the student who is able to list a minimum of ten characteristics for each of the nine planets has acquired knowledge. The learning task involved is presumably largely one of memorization.

Perception, rather than memory, is the hallmark of our comprehension category. Here, the student identifies and continues patterns. He does not do this by remembering them, but by observing them. He matches or completes equivalencies and nonequivalencies, and he perceives other relationships in material presented to him. If, for example, when given two objects, the student is able to indicate a length comparison (longer than, shorter than, same length as), he has demonstrated comprehension. Or, given a list of ten latitudes numbered in degrees, if the student is able to categorize them correctly under the headings "Region of High Temperatures," "Region of Middle Temperatures," and "Region of Low Temperatures," he has demonstrated comprehension.

For our application category, the student selects and then uses one or more principles to produce or alter something. For example, if a student decides upon and then uses a certain formula to solve a problem, he has shown that he can apply what he has learned. He works upon material according to definite rules that he perceives as being appropriate. Nevertheless, he does not go beyond these rules and principles. Initially, and as a learning task, application is a deliberate and highly conscious act, although in time it may become merely a routine operation scarcely above the threshold of awareness.

A student qualifies for our invention category when he produces, uses, or alters something in a form or manner that in some way goes beyond any existing structures or principles of which he is aware. For example, after having studied the physical structure of insects, if the student is able to construct a taxonomy of his own that consists of categories into which all of the insects studied can be sorted according to their structures, he has invented something.

Examining our haiku objective in the light of these considerations, it would seem that creative writing falls naturally into the category of invention. So let's put it there.

Taxonomy Category

Invention.

Resources are the final part of our format. What is needed here is a listing of various instructional means (tapes, films, records, filmstrips, printed matter, activities) that may be used to help students achieve the criterion performance. Resource items should not simply be assigned en masse; in each instance they should be used selectively, depending on the situation for any given student. In the case of our haiku objective:

Resources

An Introduction to Haiku (an antholology of poems and poets from Basho to Shiki, with translations and commentary by Harold G. Henderson).

Borrowed Water (a book of American haiku by the Los Altos Writers Roundtable).

American Haiku Magazine (a magazine devoted exclusively to the development of English-language haiku).

Good Night, Socrates (film).
The Red Balloon (film).
The Golden Fish (film).
The Smile (film).
Nahanni (film).
Eugene Atget (film).
Etc.

The three items of printed matter listed above provide a certain amount of background information about the nature of haiku, and some examples of this form of poetry. The film listings, which could be expanded almost indefinitely, can be used to trigger the responses of students; and when what they have to say is shaped by the discipline of haiku, the results are often gratifying and sometimes moving.

Let's take the film, *Good Night, Socrates,* as an example. In bland, diluted prose, here is how one student reacted to what she saw:

This movie was something different from anything I have ever seen. I didn't realize there are people living like that in the United States. It wasn't the condition of the buildings or anything. They weren't the best but at least they were home. It was that they lived in their own world. That boy was growing up in a totally Greek atmosphere. The people were satisfied with it too. In fact they liked it. It was very hard to be thrown out of their home and town for something like better looks. They will never live the same way again. Maybe it would have been better if they stayed that way. At least there wasn't much discrimination.

Later, in haiku, here is what this girl wrote about *Good Night, Socrates:*

> The fragile bubbles
> tremble and break before me.
> I see my world fall.

Same student, same film. The difference is due to the form of expression.

However, the pleasure of promoting haiku as a worthy exercise in the mother tongue is not to our main purpose. The point is this: We have talked at some length about the need for expressing instructional objectives in terms of observable student behavior. It would be difficult to overemphasize the importance of doing this; for, once this has been accomplished, other problems can be solved more easily. We have already indicated how this is so when it comes to the construction of test items or the selection of appropriate instructional materials and procedures. Beyond this, the usefulness of performance objectives carries over into the matter of classroom management, which, in its largest sense, is the operational problem of individualized instruction.

1234

Project Congdon

In November, 1963, the voters of Duluth passed an elementary school bond issue that, among other things, provided for the construction of a four-room addition to the Congdon Park Elementary School. The instructional program for this new addition was designed to help answer the following question: What would formal schooling be like if it seriously tried to reach the ideal of educating every child according to his own personal inventory of abilities, needs, and interests?

This was hardly a new question. In the year 1918, an observer of the educational scene put it this way:

You all know how a familiar word, persistently stared at, suddenly becomes almost alarmingly strange and meaningless—how (as William

James said) it seems to glare back from the page with no speculation in its eyes.

You will have something like the same uncanny experience if you watch the operation of a school timetable after rigorously clearing your mind of the familiar associations. From 10:15 to 11:00 twenty-five souls are simultaneously engrossed in the theory of quadratic equations; at the very stroke of the hour their interest in this subject suddenly expires, and they all demand exercise in French phonetics!

Like the agreement of actors on the stage, "their unanimity is wonderful"—but also, when one comes to think of it, ludicrously artificial. Can we devise no way of conducting our business that would bring it into better accord with the natural ebb and flow of interest and activity?*

Project Staff Members

Project Congdon got under way in the fall of 1964. Four teachers and upwards of 120 fifth and sixth graders were involved. All four teachers were volunteers. The students were the fifth and sixth graders normally in attendance at Congdon Park School. They were randomly assigned to their respective fifth and sixth grade classes, as had been customary.

Right from the start, Project Congdon abandoned the traditional arrangement of the self-contained classroom, which, it was felt, was based on the false assumption that one person, the teacher, could be all things to his pupils. As the project staff saw it, human beings do not usually have a very wide range of information. Most people, at best, generally have only one or two areas of extensive knowledge and special competence. Teachers are like almost everyone else in this respect. Because the self-contained classroom appeared to ignore this fact of life, an instructional pattern was developed that used the special strengths of the project teachers.

The original Project Congdon staff members and their teaching assignments were as follows:

John Downs, who was already teaching at Congdon Park School, became the leader of our project team. It was his responsibility to see that the over-all instructional program of Project

*T. P. Nunn, "Presidential Address to the Mathematical Association," *Mathematical Gazette*, March, 1918, as quoted in *Education on the Dalton Plan*, by Helen Parkhurst. New York: E. P. Dutton & Co., Inc., 1922, pp. xiv-xv.

Congdon was well co-ordinated, comprehensive, and effective. Four student teachers from the University of Minnesota (Duluth campus) were made directly responsible to Mr. Downs for their work within the project. In addition to this, Mr. Downs devoted himself to teaching the social studies to all of the fifth and sixth grade students.

Mrs. June Brieske had worked with first grade children for eleven years before she joined Project Congdon as a fifth and sixth grade teacher in English and art. Mrs. Brieske came to us from a neighboring school system.

Robert Shaul became our teacher of science and physical education. Like Mrs. Brieske, Mr. Shaul came to us from another school district. He had had a prior interest in team teaching as a promising approach to instruction.

Dale Koch completed the project staff. A primary grades teacher, Mr. Koch was transferred to Project Congdon from within our own school system. He was assigned major responsibility for the teaching of mathematics and music.

The four student teachers were each assigned to a single group of students, and they stayed with their group throughout the school day.

Of course, the person responsible for the operation of the entire project was our Congdon Park School principal, Mary Brown. Without her willingness to take on this task, Project Congdon would never have seen the light of day. It is the job of each principal in the Duluth Public Schools to be the instructional leader for his school. As the principal goes, so goes the program.

Finally, acting as liaison between Project Congdon and the central office of the Duluth Public Schools for the first year was William Simmons, at that time our director of special services. Mr. Simmons saw to it that the Project Congdon team had the constant and unqualified support of the central office.

Student Assignments

Student assignments were in the form of individualized lesson plans. That is to say, each student worked in each of the subject matter areas at a level and at a speed commensurate with his prior achievement and capabilities. This meant that it was perfectly possible for a given student to be working on the intricacies of different numeration systems, for example, while one of his classmates was still trying to master the multiplication table. The point was that in every subject each student was permitted to achieve as swiftly as he could, or to put it the other way around, as slowly as he had to.

Each student normally received a lesson plan designed for one week's work. This was not a hard and fast rule, however, and the anticipated working time for each lesson varied from student to student. Each lesson plan (which we called a *contract*) was typed and filed in such a manner that all students had easy access to their assignments. As a student completed one assignment, he was given another. In this way, every student was able to proceed with every subject according to his own rate of learning.

Recording Student Progress

We used Acme Visible Record Books for keeping track of student progress (*see* page 69). Each record book contained cards with grids for this purpose. For example, when a student was assigned a contract in a certain subject, his progress card for that subject was exposed and a diagonal line was drawn through the appropriate box in the grid. When the student completed his assignment, a second diagonal line was drawn to form an X in the box. This signified student accomplishment. When desired, a student score was also recorded in the box.

Measuring Student Achievement

Among other things, we used the Iowa Tests of Basic Skills to measure student achievement. These tests gave us information in the areas of vocabulary, reading comprehension, spelling, capitalization, punctuation, language usage, map reading, reading graphs and tables, knowledge and use of reference materials, arithmetic concepts, and arithmetic problem-solving. Such measurements can help receptive teachers understand the futility of putting into the hands of a fifth grade student with a third grade reading level a science or social studies book written at the fifth grade level—written, that is, at a reading level two grades beyond the student's actual reading comprehension.

Needed: More Than the Three R's

The traditional way of doing things is often a sad story indeed. Teachers work hard, for example, with certain youngsters during special periods of remedial reading instruction, which is fine, as far as it goes. But then the bell rings, and these same youngsters are immersed in other subject matter areas—at a reading level they have just demonstrated they cannot handle! Clearly, this does not make much sense. But it is understandable. In order to provide each student with the type of individualized instruction that he needs for effective learning, a wide assortment of materials and devices is required; and these things, these tools of the trade, have always been in short supply in most school systems. For our pilot project, however, we had the tools to do the job.

It was our hope, of course, that if the results of Project Congdon were encouraging enough, ways would be found to promote the development of individualized instruction throughout the entire public school system in Duluth. What results did we have in mind? Naturally, we believed that children would learn at least as much under the conditions of Project Congdon as they would in the environment of the traditional classroom. However, we were also after something more than basic academic achievement, important as that is. It was our contention that, over the years, schools had not really done a very satisfactory job of preparing students to become lifelong learners.

You have heard the familiar refrain at commencement exercises. We tell the students: "Remember, this is not an end, only a beginning." Then we say, in effect: "Okay, everybody. You're on your own. Good-by, and good luck!" Subsequently, the ones who can, and want to, go on to some further kind of schooling. But some 40 per cent of those who go on to college fail or drop out during their freshman year. The ones who don't continue their schooling—well, they get along as best they can. A growing number of them wind up unemployed, which is a far cry, certainly, from the ideal of responsible, competent, lifelong learning.

Our contention in Project Congdon was that the schools were partly responsible for this situation. We asserted that schools traditionally spend so much time supervising students that the natural curiosity of a young learner gradually becomes a dependent sort of thing, often leaning almost entirely on a steady stream of directions and exhortations from his teachers. Once this sad condition has been achieved, of course, a school could quite correctly claim that only a few of its students could be depended on to engage in independent inquiry.

We felt that an important measure of the success of Project Congdon would be the extent to which students in the project developed the ability to undertake and complete a variety of independent learning activities. It should be remembered, however, that by "independent study" we did not necessarily mean "isolated study." A student who had been given a specific instructional assignment was free to seek out and work with other students having the same assignment, or he could, if he chose, work strictly by himself. This was a matter for the student to decide. The term "independent" meant that each student had wide latitude in determining how he would complete a given assignment. He might work on it frequently for short periods of time, or he might try to work through the entire assignment at one sitting. This, again, was something that each student was encouraged to resolve for himself. Independent study did *not* mean that students were left to flounder in confusion. Regular teachers and student teachers alike were constantly available for questioning and consultation. There was little chance that individual student difficulties would go unnoticed for very long.

Characteristics of Project Congdon

The salient characteristics of Project Congdon were these:

The instruction was individualized. Students were encouraged to progress according to their own rate of learning. A large assortment of instructional materials and devices helped to make this possible. A large share of the music curriculum and almost all physical education activities, however, were taught in group situations; it made good sense to do so. *Flexibility* was the key thought behind all instructional arrangements within Project Congdon.

Although, for the most part, instruction took place on the basis of individual learning assignments and each student was, within wide limits, encouraged to decide for himself how best to complete a given assignment, tests were administered as a check on completed assignments and the progress of every student was recorded and used as a guide for further assignments.

The self-contained classroom was *not* a feature of Project Congdon. The four regular staff members exercised special responsibilities in the areas of their greatest teaching strengths. The four student teachers were each assigned to a student group, on the assumption that this would help to strengthen the instructional links between the regular teachers and the students.

The Project Congdon staff met regularly in order to co-ordinate their teaching and review the over-all progress of individual students. This co-operative planning was one of the things that set the Project Congdon program apart from the kind of departmentalized teaching that goes on in most secondary schools. Traditionally, the departmentalized secondary teacher is an isolated atom who knows very little about other parts of the instructional program. Through frequent planning sessions, the entire Project Congdon staff was well-informed on all aspects of the total program.

As might have been expected, a project of this nature, especially in its opening phases, required many hours of staff work above and beyond the usual call of duty. Indeed, the planning for Project Congdon took several months. But there was compensation for this effort in the excitement of doing something that appeared to be worth while, something that might even turn out to be significant.

Assessing Project Congdon

What assessment can be made of the first year of the project? As measured by the Iowa Tests of Basic Skills, the project students did well in the areas of vocabulary, reading comprehension, spelling, capitalization, punctuation, language usage, map reading, reading graphs and tables, knowledge and use of reference materials, arithmetic concepts, and arithmetic problem-solving. On these tests, the fifth grade students as a class scored at the 92nd percentile, and the sixth grade students scored at the 98th percentile. These gratifying results could *not*, however, be attributed solely to the particular learning environment established by the project. A control group working in a traditional self-contained classroom did just as well as the experimental group on the Iowa Tests.

The significant point is that Project Congdon not only worked effectively in promoting the basic academic achievement of the project students, but it also made it possible for these students to grow in the ability to organize their own learning activities, to become adept in acquiring the skills of independent inquiry. This was the truly exciting feature of the project; for, in the words of Richard Weatherman, Duluth's assistant superintendent in charge of pupil personnel, "This educational experiment was based on the premise that the future will demand of the educated individual that he be able to learn and relearn concepts and facts throughout his life and that these learning experiences must be self-initiated." Because this educational goal did not lend itself to measurement through conventional testing methods, we relied on teacher judgment for this important assessment. Here we can report that our Project Congdon staff members were in complete agreement that the project was effective in promoting the skills of independent inquiry. Of course, it is open to questioning whether wishful thinking significantly colored the judgment of the project staff. We are still not in a position to know. However, the feelings of the teachers were apparently shared by the mothers and fathers of our project youngsters. When the parents of our sixty graduating sixth graders were given the chance to enroll their youngsters in a follow-up individualized instruction program at Ordean Junior High School, only one child's parents declined to do so.

Inevitably, there were weaknesses in the project. For one thing, many of our student contracts, or lesson assignments, were quite pedestrian, and many failed to set forth instructional objectives in terms of student performance. Furthermore, it was not until we neared the end of the school year that we made it possible for at least a few students to suggest some of their own contracts. We felt a definite need to shape a greater number of student opportunities in this direction.

Another area in which we did little or nothing was that of educational *simulation*. The reference here is to direct student involvement in problem-solving situations that are structured as games. In constructed settings modeled after real-life situations, students have an opportunity to try out different strategies over a period of time in order to observe the consequences of their decisions. This approach to learning appears to be particularly promising in the social studies area, the field of international relations being a case in point.

Closely associated with such improvement is the matter of *process* versus *product*. Formal schooling has traditionally concerned itself almost exclusively with the *results* of scholarly inquiry rather than with the *nature* of the inquiry itself. The extent to which this state of affairs prevails is probably directly related to the number of student assignments that emphasize the simple recall or recognition of information (i.e., the taxonomy category of knowledge). Unfortunately, this is presumably the normal situation in most classrooms. Project Congdon was certainly no exception. For the most part, we were still asking students to list the principal products of Paraguay, or some such thing. From the standpoint of content, in other words, it was all too often a low-level enterprise.

Finally, although we realized that the standard report card with its ambiguous letter awards is a primitive tool hopelessly unsuited to the task of transmitting relatively precise information about the learning progress of students, we retained this traditional method of reporting to parents. Nevertheless, we were aware that we needed to devise some kind of basic skills achievement record that could be used in conjunction with a basic skills achievement catalog (or its equivalent). We also understood the importance of developing a system that would enable us to report student accomplishment of specific instructional objectives in terms of observable performance.

Comments of Outside Observers

As a general rule, the more than one thousand visitors who observed Project Congdon that first year were impressed by what they saw. Three of the many comments we received may serve as examples.

According to State Language Arts Consultant Gerald Kincaid:

I observed fifth and sixth grade pupils behaving more maturely than most college students. They were working independently without any teacher standing over them. I stopped and asked one girl what she was doing. She paused to explain clearly and succinctly the problem on which she was working. Then she went ahead with the task in a most efficient manner.

While these pupils were actively engaged with their individual projects, I saw teachers sitting down with individual pupils who needed assistance. In contrast to so many classes I have visited, I did not observe a single case of misbehavior nor a single example of a pupil idling away his time.

I observed a sixth grade boy making a report to his class on human anatomy—specifically on the human head. He was using a plastic model which could be disassembled and put back together again. He had the full attention of the class even though no teacher was in the room at the time.

Although I have no evidence in the form of test results to support my estimate, I would say that more real learning was occurring in a single day in those classes than occurs in two days in most schools I have visited. But more important, I would say they were really learning how to learn on their own, which becomes more crucial with each passing year. At the same time, individual differences were being met better than I have observed elsewhere.

Music Consultant Eunice Boardman, Associate Professor of Music Education, Wichita State University, Kansas, had this to say:

I am enclosing a copy of the recommendations which I made to the teachers engaged in the Congdon Park Project after my first visit to Duluth. I would like to emphasize the fact that I find this project one of the most exciting educational experiments that I have observed in recent years.

In terms of music development, I feel that this kind of classroom experience has certain definite advantages over the traditional musical program. In the first place learning, as you well know, is an individual process. Although music lends itself well to group participation, the specific learnings can only occur on an individual basis. I feel sure that a program where a child has the opportunity to work individually, or in small groups, to develop his musical understanding will produce results far superior to the traditional class music curriculum.

Musical participation in the adult world is almost entirely an individual or small group activity. One listens to records within his own home; he attends a concert and listens as an individual; he joins with his friends to perform music in a small ensemble, etc. Traditional musical programs in our schools do not foster this kind of participation; in contrast they continue to emphasize the kinds of skills which are useful only in large group activities: choirs, bands, orchestras. The result too often means that the young person, once out of high school and away from organized musical activities, does not know how to transfer his previous musical experience into meaningful personal recreation. I believe that a curriculum such as that developed in Duluth, carried on into the secondary schools, would help to bridge the present wide gap between existing "school music" and "adult musical life."

During my second visit to Duluth I was pleased and amazed at the progress that the teachers had made toward initiating a suitable musical curriculum. At that time I had an opportunity to examine the materials which the teachers have developed and to visit a music class. I feel that the teachers are moving toward a solution to a difficult problem. Coordinating a music program into this project requires a completely new approach to the teaching of classroom music.

My further recommendations at this time had to do with some specific suggestions toward broadening the music curriculum to include music from various periods not represented in the teacher's original outline. I had also some specific, though minor, recommendations in relation to the materials which they have developed.

I would like to say that I believe the most exciting thing which has occurred so far in the music experiment is the imagination with which the teachers have tackled the problem of developing adequate materials. The quality of these materials was excellent; they will help to fill the present materials vacuum.

My final recommendation would be to provide free time for those teachers who are working on the music program in order that they may continue to develop suitable materials and contracts. These materials will be invaluable to the Duluth music program, whether used within a project such as that of Congdon Park or as a part of a more traditional musical curriculum.

It has been most exciting to be a part of this project.

County Supervisor Fred Toman said:

Last December and several times after that I visited the Congdon School to observe the Congdon Project. The experience was a revelation in what modern education can be. Here at last I saw a system which overcomes the painful limitations of the traditional classroom and actually accomplishes individualized instruction.

I was happy to see how neatly a new approach to school organization and methods can dislodge the anachronism of the graded school, the teacher-tell-pupil routines, and the question-and-answer single-textbook rehearsals. I was equally delighted to see children fully committed to an active role in learning, taking responsibility, working diligently at their own pace, and best of all enjoying school. . . . The Congdon Project is indeed a bright light in an otherwise dull sky.

1234

FRANKLIN-NETTLETON PROJECT

One big question was raised by Project Congdon staff members and visitors alike: Would this program work with other kinds of kids? Project Congdon students, as a group, had always been high achievers. Most of these students would, if they had to, learn *in spite of* what was done to their school environment. In that sense, we had easy pickings. Now suppose the situation were reversed. Suppose we were to work with children whose school experiences had been consistently unproductive, whose academic accomplishments were significantly under par—children, in short, who could be considered educationally deprived. Would an instructional program of the Project Congdon type function effectively in this kind of setting? This was a crucial question, for on its answer would hang the fate of our plans to expand the program. The passage of the Elementary and Secondary Education Act of 1965 gave us an opportunity to answer this question. Encouraged by the prospect of being funded under Title I of the new legislation, we chose as an acid test for individualized instruction the schools of Franklin and Nettleton, where achievement scores on the Iowa Tests of Basic Skills were generally the lowest in the city. Located in Duluth's low-income Central Hillside area, both the Franklin and Nettleton schools were housed in old, traditional buildings. Franklin was constructed in 1919 as an addition to an 1888 building that was later torn down. Nettleton was built in 1905. We considered these physical factors important, because visitors to Project Congdon sometimes said that although what we were doing there looked good, such a program would not be feasible in their own schools because they had no sliding walls. We were eager to demonstrate that, though a well-designed building was indeed a blessing, individualized instruction did not necessarily stand or fall on the presence or absence of convenient facilities.

Title I Proposal

The Duluth Public Schools' Title I proposal for the Franklin-Nettleton Individualized Instruction Project was submitted to the Minnesota State Department of Education in December, 1965. It is reproduced on the pages that follow.

FRANKLIN-NETTLETON PROJECT

1. *Special education needs which this project has been designed to meet.*

This project has been designed to improve the basic academic skills of educationally deprived children residing in the low-income area served by the Franklin and Nettleton Elementary Schools. As measured by standardized achievement tests, 68 per cent of all elementary school children residing in the Franklin-Nettleton attendance area are educationally deprived.

2. *Specific objectives of the project.*

Specifically, this project will attempt to improve the achievement of educationally deprived elementary school children in the basic academic areas of vocabulary, reading comprehension, spelling, capitalization, punctuation, language usage, map reading, reading graphs and tables, knowledge and use of reference materials, arithmetic concepts, and arithmetic problem-solving.

3. *Special educational activities or services to be initiated and maintained under this project.*

This is a two-phase project. The first phase (for which monies are now sought in this application) is the *in-service* and *preparatory* phase, which is designed to take place during the period January-August, 1966. (Immediately following June 30, 1966, an application for funding the second phase of this project—the *classroom instructional* phase—will be submitted.) The first phase of the project involves (a) the hiring of personnel, (b) the acquisition of nonconsumable instructional materials and equipment, (c) the minor remodeling of classroom facilities, and (d) an extensive in-service program for teachers. The accomplishment of these items will contribute to the success of the second phase in improving the basic academic skills of the educationally deprived children participating in the project.

In-service education for teachers:

An in-service program for the project teachers will be carried on for three hours each week from January, 1966, until June, 1966, and for twenty-five hours per week for six weeks during the summer of 1966. This in-service work will include (a) studying the learning characteristics of educationally deprived children, (b) exploring improved ways of using supportive services, (c) preparing instructional objectives in terms of student performance, (d) detecting and diagnosing instructional problems for individual students, (e) selecting and organizing instructional materials in relation to specific learning needs, abilities, and interests, (f) determining appropriate means for evaluating student accomplishment, and (g) discovering better methods for reporting student progress to parents.

Acquisition of non-consumable instructional materials and equipment:

Students vary widely in their levels of achievement and in their readiness for further learning. This means that in order to provide each student with the type of individualized instruction that he needs for really effective learning, a wide assortment of materials and teaching devices is required. A competent teacher must be able to select and organize instructional materials in relation to the needs, abilities, and interests of *each one of his students* (see point (e) under *in-service education* above). Experience with Project Congdon—a pilot individualized instructional project at Congdon Park Elementary School in Duluth—indicates that an *initial* expenditure of $2,000 per classroom is needed for non-consumable instructional materials and equipment. With regard to the proposed Franklin-Nettleton Project, these items would be acquired gradually during the period January-August, 1966, as a result of careful sampling by the project teachers.

Minor remodeling of classroom facilities:

New instructional devices, kits, systems, programs, etc., are entering the educational market in an ever-increasing flow. In order to make these new products serve the goal of individualized instruction efficiently, some minor remodeling of classroom facilities is needed. Specifically, this would include (a) removing certain room partitions, (b) installing electrical outlets, darkout curtains, and viewing screens, (c) providing wardrobe facilities in corridors, and (d) installing shelving and cabinets.

Employment of personnel:

In addition to the staff members currently employed by the Duluth Public Schools, the proposed Franklin-Nettleton Project calls for the hiring of seven teacher aides, one secretary, and one regular teacher. The regular teacher is urgently needed now to relieve the situation at Franklin School where all grades, one through six, are presently split. Five of the seven teacher aides would be assigned, one aide per team, to five teaching teams within the project. Nettleton School would thus have three aides; Franklin School would have two. The remaining two aides would be assigned to serve educationally deprived youngsters on private school premises. The project will also require twelve weeks of consultant service, apportioned as follows: six weeks of service by one general consultant; six weeks of service divided as needed among special resource consultants but not to exceed in total amount the six weeks of service by the one general consultant.

The Franklin Elementary School (K-6) located at 411 East Seventh Street, and the Nettleton Elementary School (K-6) located at First Avenue East and Sixth Street, will be used in connection with this project. The Franklin School was built in 1919; the Nettleton School was built in 1905. Twelve teachers at Nettleton and six teachers at Franklin, will take part in the project. (The project information section of this application contains data on the number of children who will participate.) Because this project will take over the major portion of the total instructional program for all educationally deprived elementary school children in the project area, it would not be possible (without the construction of major new facilities) to instruct educationally deprived *private* school youngsters at either the Nettleton School or the Franklin School. Consequently, project activities for educationally deprived private school children will have to be conducted on private school premises. Specifically, this will involve the use of Sacred Heart Elementary School (1-8) located at 205 West Fourth Street. Non-consumable instructional materials and equipment will be placed in the Sacred Heart School for the duration of the project, and two teacher aides will be assigned to serve educationally deprived student in attendance there.

4. *Anticipated effectiveness of the project activities.*

It is expected that significant improvement in academic achievement will occur in the areas of vocabulary, reading comprehension, spelling, capitalization, punctuation, language usage, map reading, reading graphs and tables, knowledge and use of reference materials, arithmetic concepts, and arithmetic problem-solving. We believe this is a reasonable expectation because all of these are *basic skills* and can, therefore, be readily identified and taught. Furthermore, past experience with low-achievers has shown us that concentrated work with these youngsters usually results in more significant gains than an equal expenditure of effort upon already high-achieving children.

In order to attain the objectives listed above, it is not uncommon for school systems to initiate programs that dilute the responsibility of the regular classroom teacher for the educational progress of all students assigned to him. This point has to do with the development of various remedial programs that, in the mechanics of their operation, tend to take over the normal responsibility of the regular teacher with regard to the learning problems of certain students. *In contrast to this approach,* the Franklin-Nettleton Project will be shaped so that the regular teacher, within the regular classroom, will have full responsibility for the educational progress of all project students assigned to him. This is not to downgrade the role of special teachers, but it *is* to say that such personnel should be in a supportive role to the regular teacher and should perform their duties under the general direction of the regular teacher.

5. *Proposed procedures and techniques, including appropriate measures of educational achievement for evaluating.*

This is the initial project proposal submitted by the Duluth Public Schools. This proposal, along with other projects now being planned, constitutes the Duluth Public Schools' Title I *program* for the current fiscal year. That this over-all program is of adequate size, scope, and quality is attested to by the fact that, including the present proposal, the projects collectively provide for (a) the improvement of basic academic skills for educationally deprived elementary school children, (b) curriculum changes aimed at holding secondary school youngsters identified as potential dropouts, (c) the offering of broad experiences in art and music for educationally deprived youngsters, (d) speech therapy, social, and psychological work with children needing these special services, (e) the development of an ETV program directed at pre-school age children in low-income families, (f) the creation of a curriculum materials library designed to serve educationally deprived students, and (g) the expansion of school library services to meet the needs of low-income neighborhoods on an after-school basis.

The effectiveness of this initial project will be determined in two ways. The effectiveness of phases one and two *together* will be measured by administering the Stanford Achievement Test and the Iowa Tests of Basic Skills to the project youngsters. The Stanford Achievement Test will be given to the first and second graders. The Iowa Tests of Basic Skills will be given to the higher grades. (For purposes of assessing test results, an appropriate achievement base-line will have been established for each student beforehand.)

It must be remembered, however, that *phase one of this project* (the phase for which monies are sought in this application) is exclusively an *in-service* and *preparatory* phase, and that direct classroom instruction under the guidelines of this project will occur only during phase two, for which we will seek funding during the next fiscal year. This means that we will have to evaluate the results of the project during the *current* fiscal year *not* in terms of student achievement, but according to the *immediate* accomplishments of the *in-service* work with the project staff.

We propose to do this by determining the *total number* of *individualized lesson plans* that are developed by the project staff in preparation for phase two, the direct instructional phase. A word should be said about these individualized lesson plans. Each one will consist of three elements: (a) a specific instructional *objective,* stated in terms of student performance; (b) a sample *test* item for *measuring* accomplishment of the *objective;* and (c) several possible instructional *procedures,* one or more of which may be assigned to an *individual* student in order to help him *achieve* the desired *objective.*

Here is an example of an individualized lesson plan:

English Objective 13-C

Given twenty sentences containing a variety of mistakes in capitalization, the student is able, with at least 90 per cent accuracy, to identify and rewrite correctly each word that has a mistake in capitalization.

Sample Test Item

Look at this sentence: *"While we were waiting,"* said Tom, *"The deer came down to the lake."* If any word in the sentence is capitalized incorrectly, rewrite the word correctly. If no word in the sentence is capitalized incorrectly, write the word *none.*

Optional Instructional Procedures

——The student will work through the California Test Bureau booklet, *Capitalization,* Level C-D.

——The student will work through the California Test Bureau book-*italization.*

——The student will work through the California Test Bureau booklet, *Capitalization,* Level E-F.

——The student will attend a scheduled series of teacher-led discussions on the subject of capitalization.

——The student will study the Webster filmstrip, *Using Capital Letters.*

——The student will work through Unit 11 in *English 2200.*

——The student will work through Unit 9 in *English 2600.*

——The student will work through Lessons 87 and 88 in *English 3200.*

6. *Specific procedures and activities to be undertaken for the dissemination of significant information derived from research and demonstration projects and for the adoption of promising practices.*

Significant information concerning this and every other Title I project undertaken by the Duluth Public Schools will be disseminated by means of published reports, distributed as follows:

——Copies will be sent to every elementary and secondary school under the jurisdiction of the local educational agency.

——Copies will be sent to the Educational Research and Development Council of Northeast Minnesota.

——Copies will be placed on file with the Minnesota State Department of Education.

——Copies will be sent upon request to any interested local, state, regional, or national educational agency or organization.

Proposed Alterations at Nettleton Elementary School To Remove Room Partitions, Provide Wardrobe Facilities in Corridors, Install Shelving and Cabinets in the Teachers' Rooms, Install Darkout Curtains and Viewing Screens in All Classrooms.

Labor to remove partitions and removal of debris	$ 1,865.00
Floor patching	1,660.00
Ceiling acoustic tile repair	680.00
Plastering	917.00
General carpenter labor	1,000.00
Painting	2,215.00
Electrical work	6,100.00
Corridor wardrobes installed	2,375.00
Shelving and cabinets in teachers rooms	1,256.00
Darkout curtains	1,970.80
Viewing screens	426.25
	$20,465.05
Payroll tax and ins. @ 10.16% on $8,500.00	863.60
	$21,328.65
Supervision @ 8%	1,706.29
TOTAL............	$23,034.94

Proposed Improvements at Franklin Elementary School.

Install 5 electrical outlets in each classroom	$ 5,500.00
Install darkout curtains in all classrooms	1,094.00
Install viewing screens in all classrooms	230.00
	$ 6,824.72
Payroll tax and ins. @ 10.16% of $200 labor	20.32
	$ 6,845.04
Supervision @ 4%	273.80
TOTAL............	$ 7,118.84
GRAND TOTAL............	$30,153.78

Budget Summary

In-service

7 teacher aides @ $60 per week for 23 weeks
(Jan.-June) ....$ 9,660.00
7 teacher aides @ 37.50 per week for 6 weeks
(June-Aug.) 1,575.00
18 regular public school teachers @ $4.40 per hour
for 60 hours ($264 per teacher) (Jan.-June) 4,752.00
18 regular public school teachers @ $120 per week
for 6 weeks ($720 per teacher) (June-Aug.) 12,960.00
1 principal @ $5 per hour for 60 hours (Jan.-June) ...   300.00
1 principal @ $800 for 6 weeks (June-Aug.) 800.00
12 weeks consultant service 3,600.00

$ 33,647.00

Other

1 teacher, regular public school for 23 weeks
(Jan.-June) ($635 prorated) 3,676.31
1 secretary @ $274 per month for 5 months 1,370.00
Minor remodeling 30,153.78
Instructional materials and equipment 54,000.00

$ 89,200.09
Administrative cost (9%) 11,056.23

Grand Total............$133,903.32

In-service Program

The in-service program for the Franklin-Nettleton Project began in January, 1966. Unfortunately, we started off on the wrong foot. We decided that our first meeting should be devoted to examining a large variety of instructional materials and equipment. This was a mistake. Almost everything we saw looked good. Lacking clearly formulated instructional objectives, we were unable to sort out what was relevant from what was not. It soon became apparent that we would have to back up and begin again. We did, and concentrated on the writing of instructional objectives. This was hard work. It was difficult to think in terms of observable student behavior. Consequently, our initial progress was slow.

Preparing Objectives

Having decided that our staff members should work in the areas of their greatest subject matter strengths, as they did in Project Congdon, the task of formulating behavioral objectives in each subject area was undertaken by all the teachers who had instructional responsibilities in that subject area. This meant, for example, that our social studies teachers were responsible, as a group, for the complete layout of our social studies objectives, kindergarten through grade six.

We spent very little time questioning the content of our objectives. This does not mean that we had a high regard for the quality of our projected student learning activities. We had few illusions on that score. But we felt that it would be all we could do simply to put the old wine of the curriculum into the new bottles of criterion performance. Consequently, we accepted without much argument most of the things with which we had busied ourselves teaching in the past. It was the context rather than the content that was new. (Not until twelve months later, when we began planning for an individualized project at Chester Park Elementary School, would the problem of instructional content engage our efforts in a significant way.)

Eventually, we put together a number of objectives according to the following three-part format: criterion performance, sample test item (or situation), and instructional procedures. The following are a few examples of what we did.

LANGUAGE ARTS
(APPROXIMATE DIFFICULTY LEVEL: KINDERGARTEN)

Criterion Performance

Given three simple directions in sequence by the teacher, the student is able to follow these directions in the order given.

Sample Test Item

1. Please get the book from the shelf.
2. Bring the book to me.
3. Then sit down with the group.

Instructional Procedures

a. Teacher-led presentation.
b. *Kit a Language* (Ginn): pp. 13, 15, 106, 117, 182.
c. Worksheet LA #6.

LANGUAGE ARTS
(APPROXIMATE DIFFICULTY LEVEL: FOURTH GRADE)

Criterion Performance

Given a reading selection, with a question or statement that requires a conclusion based on the selection, and a list of several possible conclusions, the student is able to identify the correct conclusion (85 per cent accuracy).

Sample Test Item

The boys took along several flashlights and a coil of string as they started their exploration. One boy uncoiled the string as the other boy showed their way through the tunnel. Shortly before they ran out of string, they came to a large room with a pool of clear, cool water. They knew they had made an amazing discovery.

Why were the boys so amazed?
1. They had tunneled through a haystack.
2. They had followed a canyon to a lake.
3. A cave was discovered by the boys.
4. They had discovered a secret underground path.

Instructional Procedures

a. Teacher-led presentation.
b. *High Roads Workbook*: pp. 21, 26, 45, 56, 80, 96.
c. *McCall Crabbs*: Book B, Units 1-10.

SCIENCE
(APPROXIMATE DIFFICULTY LEVEL: KINDERGARTEN)

Criterion Performance

Given cubes and spheres of various sizes and textures, the student is able to construct sets of objects on the basis of color, shape, length, volume, and texture.

Sample Test Item

(A set of varied cubes and spheres.)

1. Make a set of all smooth, red cubes.
2. Find a small, green, rough cube.
3. Describe this object in two or more ways. (A rough, red sphere.)

Instructional Procedures

a. Teacher-led presentation.
b. Tape (Sci. #2) with small beads.

SCIENCE
(APPROXIMATE DIFFICULTY LEVEL: SECOND GRADE)

Criterion Performance

Given a meter stick and two distances to be measured, the student is able to compare distances first by walking a designated number of steps and then measuring the same distance with the meter stick.

Sample Test Item

1. Compare the length and width of the room by measuring it in steps and with a meter stick. (It is 25 steps wide and 50 steps long. It is 10 sticks wide and 20 sticks long.)
2. What can you tell us from these measurements? (The room is longer than it is wide.)

Instructional Procedures

a. Teacher-led presentation.
b. Film *Let's Measure: Inches, Feet, Yards*, #490.
c. Filmstrip: *How Long Is It?* (Measuring).

SOCIAL STUDIES
(APPROXIMATE DIFFICULTY LEVEL: FOURTH GRADE)

Criterion Performance

Given 20 slides showing important points of interest in Duluth, a random list of their names, and a list of reasons why each is important, the student is able to put the number of each slide in front of the correct name for each and the letter of the reason why each is important after the name of that point of interest.

Sample Test Item

Look at each slide carefully. Place the number of the slide in front of the name for each point of interest. When you have finished the slides put the correct letter of the reason why each point of interest is important after the number of each point of interest.

———Statue of Sieur Duluth

———Duluth Arena-auditorium

A. New sports center completed in August, 1966.

B. The first explorer to leave a record that he was at the present location of our city.

Instructional Procedures

a. Teacher-led presentation.

b. Programmed book and tape #74-3, *Points of Interest in Duluth.*

c. Work Sheet #74-3C.

SOCIAL STUDIES
(APPROXIMATE DIFFICULTY LEVEL: FOURTH GRADE)

Criterion Performance

Given a lettered list of the names of the countries of the British Isles (England, Scotland, Wales, Ireland) and a series of 20 statements describing living conditions in these areas, the student is able to place the letter or letters of the countries in front of the statements that apply (80 per cent accuracy).

Sample Test Item

Place the letter or letters of the countries in front of the statements that apply to those countries.

A. England

B. Scotland

C. Ireland

———A large part of this country has a very small population.

———This country has many heavy industries.

Instructional Procedures

a. Teacher-led presentation.

b. Work Sheet #74-10B.

c. Listen to tape #74-10, *Living Conditions in the British Isles,* and complete the study sheet.

MATHEMATICS
(APPROXIMATE DIFFICULTY LEVEL: SECOND GRADE)

Criterion Performance

Given a set of three numerals that name whole numbers not greater than six, the student is able to list the four related addition and subtraction equations suggested by the numbers.

Sample Test Item

List the four related addition and subtraction equations suggested by the numerals 2, 3, and 1.

Instructional Procedures

a. The student will attend a teacher-led presentation based on pp. 1-4, 47-48 in *Mathematics for the Elementary School,* Book 2 (Teacher's Commentary), revised edition, SMSG, and compute the answers to all exercises on pp. 21-22 in the Student's Text.

b. The student will attend a teacher-led presentation based on pp. 33, 45, 56 in *Elementary Mathematics, Patterns and Structure,* Book 2, (Teacher's Edition), and compute the answers to all exercises on pp. 33, 45, 56 in the Student's Text.

MATHEMATICS
(APPROXIMATE DIFFICULTY LEVEL: THIRD GRADE)

Criterion Performance

Given ten finite sets, the student is able to name the number of each set with 100 per cent accuracy.

Sample Test Situation

Name the number of set A.

$A = \{$Monday, Tuesday, Wednesday, Thursday, Friday$\}$
$n(A) = \square$

Instructional Procedures

a. The student will study and work through the development sections and compute the answers to all exercises on pp. 4-8 in *Mathematics for the Elementary School,* Book 4, Part I, revised edition, SMSG.

b. The student will study and work through the development sections and compute the answers to all exercises on pp. 5-11 in *Elementary Mathematics—Patterns and Structure*, Book 3, Nichols and others.

c. Teacher-led presentation.

Need for Instructional Variety

The lack of variety among instructional procedures was (and continues to be) one of our biggest problems. It was (and is) almost impossible to find a suitable range of commercially available materials that could be used in assisting students to achieve desired objectives. Not only are there virtually no instructional materials now in existence that define in any measurable way what it is that they can help students learn, but multi-media instructional packages with multi-level capabilities are, for all practical purposes, unobtainable in the current educational market. For example, the child with a reading problem is frequently penalized in other academic areas because neither appropriate printed matter at an easier reading level nor relevant information in a different format (films, tapes, records, etc.) can be secured. This situation is both commonplace and tragic. Unfortunately, there is no immediate relief in sight.

Organizing Objectives

Our Franklin-Nettleton Project difficulties with materials were compounded because of the specificity of our objectives. More accurately, perhaps, we became aware of such difficulties sooner than we might have in a traditional program, where mere ground-covering is so often the order of the day. In any case, we organized our performance objectives in a series of booklets color-coded and numbered to indicate the approximate grade level of the objectives within each booklet. The number of objectives we had for mathematics, science, language arts, and social studies is shown in the table on page 41.

Within any given booklet, there were substantial differences in size and complexity among our objectives. This was not so much deliberate as it was accidental. We simply did not know how large an instructional objective should be. On the one hand, we wanted our objectives to be small enough so that each student

	Mathematics	Science	Language Arts	Social Studies
Booklet K 13		18	57	39
Booklet One 62		20	69	50
Booklet Two 67		20	56	40
Booklet Three 66		19	55	43
Booklet Four 67		15	65	55
Booklet Five 70		19	67	50
Booklet Six 70		22	68	58
Total Objectives 415		133	437	335

would be able to feel a solid sense of accomplishment within the framework of his personal attention span, and so that the teachers would be able to pinpoint student difficulties quickly whenever they might arise. On the other hand, we did not want our objectives to be so small that teachers would have little time to do anything except check out students on the attainment of objectives. Furthermore, we had to recognize that what one student might reasonably hope to achieve in a week, another student might easily accomplish in a day. We found no easy solutions to this problem.

At one point, we made an attempt to develop curriculum maps that would show relationships among our objectives. An example of such a map is given on page 42. The numbered circles on the map represent instructional objectives, and their placement from left to right suggests a desirable instructional sequence. The lines connecting some of the circles show relationships of dependency as they may exist among instructional objectives. The placement of the circles from top to bottom indicates that these objectives have been classified according to Bloom's cognitive categories of knowledge, comprehension, application, analysis, synthesis, and evaluation.

Perhaps the most significant thing to emerge from our work with these maps was the realization that the sequencing of subject matter may have more flexibility in fact than it sometimes has in theory. Note how many of the objectives on our Language Arts Series 71 (our first grade level) Curriculum Map can apparently be taught without any *necessary* reference to other objectives. (The black circles simply represent points of convergence,

KNOWLEDGE

COMPREHENSION

APPLICATION

ANALYSIS

SYNTHESIS

EVALUATION

Curriculum Map
Language Arts
Series 71
Franklin-Nettleton Project
School Year 1966-67

and are not separate objectives in themselves.) For example, the map suggests that Objectives 4 and 5 would have to be mastered before either Objective 21 or Objective 22 could be attained. However, Objectives 6 through 20 could, according to our map, be tackled without regard to Objectives 4 and 5. The dotted vertical line means that we felt the first forty-one objectives should be mastered before efforts were made to achieve the others.

In order that you may judge for yourself the truth of our assertions concerning the *lack* of dependency relationships among objectives, all of the criterion performance statements for the Language Arts Series 71 objectives are set forth below. Study them in whatever way you wish, including our placement of them on the map. (We were equally surprised to note that our mathematics objectives, although somewhat more closely tied together, were also far from being the tightly-knit group that educators sometimes suppose.)

LANGUAGE ARTS
SERIES 71
Franklin-Nettleton Project
School Year 1966-67

Outline of Skills	Objectives
I. Reading	
A. Readiness.	1-8
B. Vocabulary.	
1. Word recognition.	9-17
2. Word meaning.	18-20
C. Word analysis.	
1. Phonics.	21-33
2. Structural analysis.	34-41
D. Comprehension.	42-54
II. English.	
A. Punctuation.	55-58
B. Capitalization.	59-60
C. Creative writing.	61
D. Reference skills.	62
III. Spelling and Writing.	63-69

Preparation Team

Myrtle A. Erickson, Bernice V. Gunderson, and Kathleen A. Kobus

Criterion Performance Statements

I. Reading.

A. Readiness.

1. Given two sets of alphabet cards, the student is able to match the lower-case letter with the upper-case letter having the same name (80 per cent accuracy).

2. Given alphabet letters, 26 upper-case letters and 26 lower-case letters, the student is able to name them correctly (80 per cent accuracy).

3. Given orally several sets of three words, two of which rhyme, the student is able to name the rhyming pair in each set (90 per cent accuracy).

4. Given words pronounced in groups of three, two of which begin with the same sound, the student is able to select the two words that begin with the same sound (90 per cent accuracy).

5. Given words pronounced in groups of three, two of which end with the same sound, the student is able to select the two having endings that sound alike (90 per cent accuracy).

6. Given several sets of four words arranged horizontally, three being identical words and one being different from the others, the student is able to cross out the one that is different (90 per cent accuracy).

7. Given a story orally, the student is able to provide an original title according to the information given in the story.

8. Given pictures comprising a story, the student is able to place the pictures in correct left-to-right time sequence.

B. Vocabulary.

B-1. Word recognition.

9. Given, in groups of three, sight words including those listed below, the student is able to circle the word pronounced from each group (85 per cent accuracy).

the	blue	by	airplane
he	to	green	come

find	from	away	yellow
do	first	want	good
have	down	for	go
are	apple		

10. Given, in groups of three, sight words including those listed below, the student is able to circle the word pronounced from each group (85 per cent accuracy).

mother	father	boy	something
girl	baby	toy	grandmother
dog	duck	pig	grandfather
horse	cow	oh	policeman
surprise	good-by	like	birthday

11. Given, in groups of three, sight words including those listed below, the student is able to circle the word pronounced from each group (85 per cent accuracy).

help	cookies	hide	party
please	her	in	little
not	pretty	here	jump
look	now	run	how
out	make	one	we
new	where		

12. Given, in groups of three, sight words including those listed below, the student is able to circle the word pronounced from each group (85 per cent accuracy).

said	put	ride	saw
see	table	white	brown
two	splash	three	four
soon	stop	funny	there
was	you	very	thank

13. Given, in groups of three, sight words including those listed below, the student is able to circle the word pronounced from each group (85 per cent accuracy).

about	every	know	sleep
because	five	long	take
but	eight	many	today
came	hot	off	upon
does	just	read	wash

14. Given, in groups of three, sight words including those listed below, the student is able to circle the word pronounced from each group (85 per cent accuracy).

after	been	by	carry
done	fall	give	grow
hold	keep	near	under
may	old	open	right
shall	tell	these	light
were			

15. Given, in groups of three, sight words including those listed below, the student is able to circle the word pronounced from each group (85 per cent accuracy).

your	write	warm	use
try	so	round	pull
our	never	Mr.	Mrs.
myself	made	hurt	going
full	far	draw	cut
around	better		

16. Given, in groups of three, sight words including those listed below, the student is able to circle the word pronounced from each group (85 per cent accuracy).

again	before	both	clean
cold	don't	fly	from
gave	kind	must	once
own	pick	show	some
their	those	who	work

17. Given, in groups of three, sight words including those listed below, the student is able to circle the word pronounced from each group (85 per cent accuracy).

always	any	ate	buy
could	found	goes	only
or	start	together	over
laugh	why	would	eat
much	farm	house	three

B-2. Word meaning.

18. Given a list of words, each word followed by three words, one of which is its antonym, the student is able to circle the correct antonym for each word on the list (80 per cent accuracy).

19. Given a list of words, each word followed by three words, one of which is its synonym, the student is able to underline the correct synonym (80 per cent accuracy).

20. Given a list of words, each word followed by three words, one of which is its homonym, the student is able to circle the correct homonym (80 per cent accuracy).

C. Word analysis.

C-1. Phonics.

21. Given, in groups of three, words containing the consonant elements "m," "n," "p," "f," and "th," and the short vowels "a" and "i," the student is able to circle the word pronounced in each group (80 per cent accuracy).

22. Given, in groups of three, words containing the consonant elements "c," "s," "b," "ng," "sh," "d," "g," and "h," and the short vowels "a" and "i," the student is able to circle the word pronounced in each group (80 per cent accuracy).

23. Given, in groups of three, words containing the consonant elements "r," "ch," "k," and "l," the short vowel "e," and any sounds previously taught, the student is able to circle the word pronounced in each group (80 per cent accuracy).

24. Given, in groups of three, words containing the consonant elements "v," "w," "x," "y," "z," and sounds previously taught, the student is able to circle the word pronounced in each group (80 per cent accuracy).

25. Given, in groups of three, words containing the final silent "b," final "ir," and "al," "j," "ar," final "y," the long vowel "e," and sounds previously taught, the student is able to circle the word pronounced in each group (80 per cent accuracy).

26. Given, in groups of three, words containing the final "ay," the short sound of "u," and sounds previously taught, the student is able to circle the word pronounced in each group (80 per cent accuracy).

27. Given orally a list of one-syllable words containing long vowel sounds, the student is able to write the vowel letter and mark the vowel letter long or short according to the sound heard in the word (80 per cent accuracy).

28. Given orally a list of one-syllable words containing short vowel sounds, the student is able to write the

vowel letter and mark the vowel letter long or short according to the sound heard in the word (80 per cent accuracy).

29. Given orally a list of words that begin with consonant blends—"st," "tr," "br," "cr," "dr," "fr," "gr," "pr," "bl," "cl," "fl," "gl," "pl," "sl," "sp," "sn," "sm," "sc," "sk," "sw," "tw," "thr," "squ," "scr," "spr," "shr," "spl," "dw," "sch," "str"—the student is able to write the correct initial blend for each word pronounced (80 per cent accuracy).

30. Given orally a list of words containing consonant digraph—"ch," "sh," "wh," "th," "nk," "ph," "ck,"—the student is able to write the correct digraph heard in each word pronounced (80 per cent accuracy).

31. Given orally a list of words beginning with a single consonant, the student is able to write the correct initial consonant for each word (80 per cent accuracy).

32. Given orally a number of words having a consonant in medial position, the student is able to write the correct medial consonant for each word pronounced (80 per cent accuracy).

33. Given orally a number of words ending in any consonant, the student is able to write the correct final consonant for each word pronounced (90 per cent accuracy).

C-2. Structural analysis.

34. Given word pairs, one of which has the suffix "s," the student is able to select the word pronounced in each pair (85 per cent accuracy).

35. Given word pairs, one of which has the suffix "ing," the student is able to select the word pronounced in each pair (85 per cent accuracy).

36. Given word pairs, one of which has the suffix "ed," the student is able to select the word pronounced in each pair (85 per cent accuracy).

37. Given one-syllable words containing the short vowel sound, the student is able to add correctly the ending "s," "ed," or "ing" (80 per cent accuracy).

38. Given a list of one-syllable, long-vowel words ending in "e," the student is able to drop the final "e" and add the suffix "s," "ed," or "ing" (80 per cent accuracy).

39. Given words ending in "ed" (*id,* as in "handed," and *t,* as in "skipped"), the student is able to pronounce each word correctly.

40. Given a list of words that end with the suffix "s," "ed," or "ing," the student is able to write the root word from which each word was made (90 per cent accuracy).

41. Given two lists of one-syllable words, the student, by selecting one word from each list, is able to form correctly each of the compound words (85 per cent accuracy).

D. Comprehension.

42. Given paragraphs at 1^1 level and three sentences below each paragraph, the student is able to number the sentences sequentially as they happened in the paragraph (80 per cent accuracy).

43. Given paragraphs at 1^2 level and three sentences below each paragraph, the student is able to number the sentences sequentially as they happened in the paragraph (80 per cent accuracy).

44. Given a paragraph presented orally and a list of written sentences pertaining to details in the paragraph, based upon information in the paragraph, the student is able to give correct "yes" and "no" answers to each sentence (80 per cent accuracy).

45. Given a paragraph presented orally and a list of three main ideas provided by the teacher, based on facts in the paragraph, the student is able to select the correct main idea (80 per cent accuracy).

46. Given a paragraph to be read silently and a list of written sentences pertaining to details in the paragraph, based upon information given in the paragraph, the student is able to give correct "yes" or "no" answers to each sentence (80 per cent accuracy).

47. Given a paragraph to be read silently and a list of three main ideas provided by the teacher, based upon facts in the paragraph, the student is able to select the correct main idea (80 per cent accuracy).

48. Given a series of word definitions and three words following each definition, the student is able to select the word that fits the particular definition (80 per cent accuracy).

49. Given paragraphs to which a conclusion or prediction must be supplied, the student is able to select the most logical conclusion or prediction from each paragraph.

50. Given several paragraphs at the 1^1 level and a list of three titles provided by the teacher below each paragraph, the student is able to select from three choices the title that is the subject of most or all of the sentences (80 per cent accuracy).

51. Given several paragraphs at the 1^2 level and a list of three titles provided by the teacher below each paragraph, the student is able to select from the three choices the title that is the subject of most or all of the sentences (80 per cent accuracy).

52. Given a story, the student is able to retell the principal details of the story in proper sequence.

53. Given a story, in a group situation, the student is able to acceptably dramatize his role or roles according to ideas presented in the story.

54. Given a story, based on information in the story, the student is able to construct a picture to illustrate his understanding and interpretation of the story.

II. English.

A. Punctuation.

55. Given groups of words, some statements and some questions, the student is able to insert periods and question marks correctly (90 per cent accuracy).

56. Given sentences, some containing plural nouns and some containing nouns needing an apostrophe to show possession, the student is able to correctly place an apostrophe with those nouns that show possession and to write the complete sentence (80 per cent accuracy).

57. Given a short story containing periods, question marks, exclamation marks, quotation marks, and commas, the student, when reading orally, is able to show awareness of the punctuation by using voice inflection.

58. Given sentences containing direct quotations, the student is able to underline the words of the direct quotation (80 per cent accuracy).

B. Capitalization.

59. Given a list of words, some of which are proper nouns, the student is able to capitalize those words that are proper nouns (80 per cent accuracy).

60. Given groups of words, some phrases and some sentences, the student is able to correctly place capitals at the beginning of those words that make a sentence and write the complete sentence (85 per cent accuracy).

C. Creative writing.

61. Given the background information for writing each of the items listed below, and the motivation for creative writing, the student is able to write originally each of the following:
    a. A sentence.
    b. A paragraph.
    c. A story.
    d. A poem.

D. Reference skills.

62. Given a list of words in random order, the student is able to arrange these words in alphabetical order according to the beginning letter of each word (90 per cent accuracy).

III. Spelling and Writing.

63. Given an oral dictation of the alphabet letters in random order, the student is able to print the lower-case and upper-case symbols in the acceptable manuscript form.

64. Given dictated sentences, the student is able to write, spell, and space the words correctly (80 per cent accuracy).

65. Given certain dictated words containing the consonant elements "m," "p," "n," "t," "th," and "f," and the short vowels "a" and "i," the student is able to write the words in correct manuscript form and spell them correctly (80 per cent accuracy).

66. Given certain words containing the consonant elements "s," "b," "ng," "h," "sh," "d," and "g," and any sounds previously taught, the student is able to write the words in correct manuscript form and spell them correctly (80 per cent accuracy).

67. Given certain words containing the consonant elements "ch," "k," and "l," the short vowel "e," and any sounds previously taught, the student is able to write the words in correct manuscript form and spell them correctly (80 per cent accuracy).

68. Given certain dictated words containing the consonant elements "w," "v," "x," "z," final "ay," the short vowel "u," and any sounds previously taught, the student is able to write the words in correct manuscript form and spell them correctly (80 per cent accuracy).

69. Given by dictation certain words containing the elements "al," "j," "ar," final silent "b," final "ir," final "y," the long vowel "e," and sounds previously taught, the student is able to write the words in correct manuscript form and spell them correctly (80 per cent accuracy).

Fighting Instructional Segregation

The Franklin-Nettleton Project offered us an opportunity to challenge the growing fragmentation of classroom instruction. To an ever-increasing extent, it seems, the "regular" classroom teacher professes himself unable to work effectively with youngsters who are not "average." If a student has a reading problem, he is, as likely as not, dispatched to a reading clinic. If he is "too bright," a separate class for gifted students awaits his presence. If he is "too slow," a special class for mentally retarded students is his fate. Logically, educators with an individualized approach to instruction must reject such arrangements. In the Franklin-Nettleton Project, we did.

Our most notable reversal of the fragmentation of classroom instruction involved fourteen educable mentally retarded students. Although these students resided within the established attendance areas for the Franklin and Nettleton schools, they would, in the normal course of events, have been assigned to special education classes elsewhere in the district. Instead of being shipped off to this kind of segregated educational environment, these children were assigned to classes with their regular age-peer groups within the project. In other words, the ten-year-old educable mentally retarded child was scheduled to work throughout the school day with the other fifth grade students. He would not, of course, be doing "fifth grade" work. He would be working (hopefully, with success) at whatever level of achievement his capabilities might permit.

The decision to include educable mentally retarded students within the regular instructional framework of the project initially caused a certain amount of anxiety among our project staff members. This was understandable. The effect produced by a low intelligence quotient, arbitrary and unreliable as it is, upon the attitude of an educator who has seen it is truly remarkable. It is almost as though the fateful declaration (I.Q. under 70!) were written in stone. Immediately, stereotyped images parade through his mind. It becomes impossible for him to see how, as an educator, he can be expected to teach pupils of such limited abilities, particularly when these youngsters are mixed in with students of greater academic power. If pessimism proceeds far enough, the whole business turns out to be a self-fulfilling prophecy, with "I told you so!" as the final exclamation.

Fortunately, despite some early misgivings, our project teachers were willing to accept the implications of what we were trying to do. A resource teacher was added to the staff as a replacement for the special education teacher who ordinarily would have worked with our retarded pupils in a separate environment. The job of the resource teacher, it must be emphasized, was *not* to set up a special education class within the project. Nor was she even to assume primary responsibility for the EMR students. The task of educating these students was to be undertaken by the regular classroom teacher with *appropriate support* from the resource teacher. By "appropriate support" is meant: (1) assistance in the form of information concerning the capabilities of each EMR child assigned to the regular teacher, (2) recommendations regarding the availability and use of promising instructional materials and procedures, and (3) some tutorial work with the EMR children within the normal classroom setting—but only as specifically requested by the regular teacher.

The increasing tendency of school systems to fragmentize their instructional programs will not be checked until regular classroom teachers are both willing and able to assume general responsibility for educating all the students assigned to their care.

Elementary Counseling

In order to strengthen the Franklin-Nettleton Project, the Duluth Public Schools hired (for the first time) an elementary counselor and assigned him to the project. His responsibilities were many. Much of his time was devoted to working directly with students, both individually and in small groups. His attention to the problems of individual students frequently brought him into the classroom. There he would sit and converse with children about their academic concerns as well as their personal problems. His province was nothing less than the realm of values. Working with teachers, the counselor was then able to bring his own special perspective to bear on the task of assembling and interpreting information regarding the strengths and weaknesses of individual youngsters.

Meetings with parents were an important part of the elementary counselor's duties. These meetings involved not only pupil progress reporting, but group tours of the project during which the over-all program was explained and give-and-take discussions encouraged. In addition to this, the counselor made himself available to educators from other schools so that our experiences might be shared with them. At a conservative estimate, more than a thousand visitors came to observe the Franklin-Nettleton Project during its first year of operation.

Teacher Aides

Besides a resource teacher and an elementary counselor, the project also employed teacher aides. As the name implies, the job of a teacher aide is to aid the teacher. But how? Should a teacher aide be more than a clerk? Should a properly-trained teacher aide be able to perform limited *instructional* tasks under the general supervision of the classroom teacher? We finally decided to answer these questions affirmatively, but the decision wasn't an easy one to make. The following statement (September, 1965) from the State Department of Education concerning the employment of teacher aides in Minnesota public schools shows why:

The primary purpose of teacher aides is to increase the effectiveness of the teacher in the classroom. If a plan is to be set up for the use of these aides, it is important to determine the nature of the duties to be performed. Are they to do purely clerical and housekeeping tasks, or will they devote part of their time to assisting with the teaching function? If the former, noncertificated personnel can be employed. If the latter, the aide becomes a teacher. State statutes require that teachers must be certificated. The matter of primary concern here is not certification itself, but the fact that certification implies preparation for teaching. Persons who perform professional, or even semi-professional duties, must be properly prepared for them. While certification does not guarantee a successful teacher, it does attest to the completion of a program of preparation.

The prospect of having noncertificated personnel encroach upon the prerogatives of the regular teaching staff is certainly cause for legitimate concern. However, we felt that before any work that consisted of "assisting with the teaching function" was automatically classified taboo for teacher aides, we ought to examine briefly what it is that teacher education programs uniquely qualify our regular teachers to do.

In theory, at least, schools of education turn out teachers who are able to *arrange the formal learning environment* in such a way that the goals of instruction are met. The essential point is that the competent teacher must be capable of making certain kinds of *decisions*. The range and level of this decision-making are what define the effective role of the classroom teacher. To be more specific, a well-prepared teacher should be able to *determine* whether a certain instructional item might be usefully presented to a given student. The teacher does not necessarily need to be able to *create* this item. The instructional material itself is normally available through books, films, records, tapes, filmstrips, and so forth. That is what these commercially prepared materials are for.

There is a common tendency to confuse teaching with producing and presenting. This attitude fosters a situation in which the height of imagination is finding yet another way to chain some new marvel of communication to the presence of an educational broadcaster—to limit new media to what is essentially nothing more than the traditional lecture method all decked out in mechanical finery. A particularly depressing example of this is instructional television, All too often, television instruction consists of taped lectures in which the camera is obediently fixed on the speaker's mouth as it opens and closes on selected morsels of wisdom.

As long as teaching is equated with specific overt activity, we shall spend a lot of time trying to decide which physical acts, in themselves, constitute teaching and which do not. The likely upshot of this will be the formulation of lists of approved and disapproved tasks for which teacher aides can be used. It would be difficult to suggest a more barren approach to the job of instruction.

Can we suppose, for example, that only the regular teacher should present any given body of information to a group of students? If so, what happens to the long-standing practice of using community resource persons to enrich the instructional program? Indeed, what happens to films, books, and other prime means of presenting information to students?

Can we reasonably maintain that the regular teacher is the only one qualified to hear a child read the Dolch list of the 95 most common nouns, read to children, help students locate materials, repeat directions concerning assignments, and so on? Hardly. A competent teacher aide could do all of these things, each task clearly having the effect of "assisting with the teaching function."

We finally concluded that the distinguishing characteristic of the qualified teacher is his ability to *analyze* the instructional needs of his students and *prescribe* the elements of formal schooling that will best meet those needs. On this basis, it is altogether proper for the teacher aide to be more than a clerical aide. The usefulness of the teacher aide should be restricted only by his own personal limitations in whatever duties may be assigned to him by the regular classroom teacher.

Describing the Franklin-Nettleton Project

The 1966-67 school year began officially on September 7, 1966. (It had been preceded by a trial run during the latter part of August.) This is how staff writer Delores Orman reported what she had seen for the Duluth *Herald*:*

There have been some changes made at Franklin and Nettleton elementary schools.

*September 26, 1966.

The more than 500 children attending the two schools have been experiencing a new approach to education since they began classes September 7.

Individualized instruction is the formal name of the new project. From the pupils point of view the task of learning has become more fun. It has meant learning to work filmstrip projectors and other machines, working in self-testing books, passing to different rooms to complete their own special assignments and in general more freedom than in the traditional classroom situation.

For faculty members and school officials it has become an opportunity to give individual help to each pupil according to his capacity, to tailor assignments to the students needs, and to help the student advance at his own rate of learning.

The Nettleton-Franklin project is quite similar to the Congdon Park school project, which is now into its third year.

But the new program is being carried out at all grade levels, kindergarten through sixth grade, and not just in the 5th and 6th grades as is the case at Congdon.

Educable mentally retarded children from the Franklin-Nettleton area also are participating in the project. Children are placed with their own age group, but the educational materials they use are geared to their own learning capacity.

Several children in the Franklin-Nettleton area got an advanced taste of the new program when they were selected at random to participate in a pre-September session August 22-26 at Nettleton school.

Faculty members and school officials had been working since early January preparing for the project, planning and outling the program and subject matter and selecting the teaching materials.

Then it was time for a trial run to iron out any bugs. In mid-July, the children were selected at random on the basis of parents who, in a questionnaire, had expressed an interest in having their children participate in the trial run. About 10 children were selected from each grade. Fifteen teachers from the Franklin and Nettleton schools participated.

The classes were conducted from 9 to 11 a.m. daily. The subject areas included language arts (spelling, English, penmanship, reading), science, social studies, art, music and physical education. A teacher was responsible for one or more of the subject areas.

The children were grouped into two class divisions; one through third grade and the other fourth through sixth grades.

Individual pupil assignments were based on the results of tests on basic skills given during the school year. Through the pre-tests, school officials were able to determine each pupil's deficiencies and plan a program that would concentrate on these areas whether it be in mathematics or map reading.

After being given assignments in the various subjects, pupils pursued the completion of the projects at their own rate, moving freely from one room to another. Their progress was measured by tests on the studied material. Nettleton-Franklin Principal John Downs, who was a teaching team leader at Congdon Park, explained that one of the goals of the new instruction method is to develop a sense of responsibility in the child.

In the present school program, there are 12 teachers at Nettleton, which has an enrollment of about 420. Six instructors handle the lower group, which includes kindergarten through third grade, and six are handling the upper group. The teachers are assisted by three teacher aides.

At Franklin school, which has an enrollment of about 142, three teachers handle the kindergarten through second grade and three the third through sixth grades. There are two teacher aides at the school.

Both schools utilize the services of a counselor.

During the pre-September session, both pupils and faculty expressed enthusiasm and excitement over the new method. Many pupils preferred it to the old system.

"It's a lot of fun and it's easier," Debbie Osberg, one of the participating children, said. "You learn more. Our teacher said you learn more if it's easier."

Timmy McDowell also expressed enjoyment. He said he liked "going from room to room and teacher to teacher" and "books that check yourself."

Mrs. Bernice Gunderson, language arts teacher at Nettleton, a participant in the tryout, said, "We agree that it would be hard to go back into the old system. The enthusiasm is so great. The important thing now is to get started."

Started it has. The project is financed by funds under Title I of the Elementary and Secondary Education Act of 1965.

About $138,000 was approved for the Franklin-Nettleton project last December. A major portion of that amount, more than $24,000, was budgeted. Most of the remodeling occurred at Nettleton where interior walls were removed to produce larger rooms.

Additional electrical outlets were installed at both schools.

The major portion of the remaininng funds was budgeted for the purchase of instructional and guidance supplies, textbooks and library books, and other instructional equipment.

About 14.8 per cent of the Franklin-Nettleton project funds were allotted to Sacred Heart Catholic school where a similar project is being conducted.

Applications for funds for another year of operation are expected to be approved by the State Department of Education.

Individualized instruction can be carried on in old school buildings. This is Nettleton School. Built in 1905, it is a traditional physical plant in every respect except one: some of the walls unnecessary for support have been removed to facilitate a team approach to individualized instruction.

This interior scene at Nettleton shows how two classrooms have been connected through the removal of a wall. Since Nettleton is in a low-income neighborhood, it has been eligible for Title I funds, which have been used to support the minor remodeling of classroom spaces.

Characteristics of the Franklin-Nettleton Project

Staff Organization

As mentioned earlier, project teachers were assigned subject matter responsibilities in the areas of their greatest professional interests and competencies. This did not mean that a teacher might not work with a child in several subject matter areas, but that each teacher would have certain areas in which he was *primarily* responsible for the educational development of the children assigned to his project team. It was merely another way of affirming that not everyone can, effectively, have equal responsibilities for everything. A division of labor simply makes good sense.

By the end of the school year, the line-up for the project was:

STAFF MEMBERS	ASSIGNMENTS
Dwight Rindahl	Counselor at both schools.
Mrs. Patricia Ostrom	Resource person at Nettleton, music and chorus at Franklin, music Grades 2 and 3 at Nettleton.

Franklin School

Upper Team	Terence Churchill	Team Leader, mathematics, science, police patrol.
	Mrs. Mary Jo King	Language arts, music.
	Thomas Ogston	Social studies, physical education.
Primary Team	Mrs. Kathryn Hays	Team Leader, kindergarten, science, art, physical education.
	Karen Kloepfel	Social studies, language arts, music.
	Kathleen Kobus	Mathematics, language arts, music.

Nettleton School

Upper Team	Robert Plachecki	Team Leader, mathematics.
	James Baird	Art, science.
	Richard Peterson	Language arts, music, chorus.
	Mrs. Betty Rudeseal	Social studies.
	Laurence Ruppel	Science, physical education.
	H. LeRoy Southworth	Language arts.
Primary Team	Mrs. Bernice Gunderson..	Team Leader, language arts, art.
	Richard Colin	Science, physical education, art.
	Mrs. Myrtle Erickson.....	Language arts, art.
	Carol Spreitzer	Social studies, mathematics, art.
	Peggy Staubs............	Social studies, science, mathematics, art, music, physical education.
Kindergarten	Dorothy Beerhalter	Kindergarten (afternoon).
	Mrs. Florence Brown	Kindergarten.

Scheduling

Although the youngsters in the primary grades were on a fixed time schedule for their various subjects, the students in the upper grades were, for the most part, *self-scheduled*. With the exception of physical education and music, each student in the upper grades was free to decide for himself when and for how long he would work with any given subject. If he chose, for example, to spend most of Monday working on a science experiment, he could do so. Of course, in the long run, he was obligated to complete all of his assignments (contracts) in all of his subjects, and to do this according to the requirements of each contract. But within these blocks of time, he could make his own decisions about what matters to pursue. It was gratifying to observe how well fourth, fifth, and sixth grade youngsters were able to manage their own activities.

Grouping

Flexibility was the keynote in grouping students. At any given time, in any given room, students at different grade levels and of varying degrees of intellectual power might be working together, or at least side by side. Fourth, fifth, and sixth grade youngsters moved easily among each other, and an educable mentally retarded child might be studying next to the pupil who was academically most able. In this kind of setting, student groups formed and dissolved through the free selection of the youngsters themselves or for the specific instructional purposes of the teachers. Selections and purposes were, in turn, generally based upon the performance criteria of student contracts. Although each pupil worked at his own rate and in his own way upon his own objectives, at any point in time there would usually be a number of students working on the same contract, which made it possible for groups to form on the basis of common objectives. This is what happened in the normal course of events. The difference between this flexible way of grouping for instruction and that relatively meaningless group called "the class" in the traditional school is enormous. Indeed, this "difference" makes all the difference in the world.

Student Work Assignments

It would be nice to report that the matter of assigning work to students was clearly thought out, that student needs were precisely analyzed and assignments made accordingly. But this was not the case. For any subject, the necessary, even desirable, scope and sequence of learning that is assumed to exist may not really exist—at least not in the neatly compartmentalized form that is sometimes imagined. In lieu of dependable curriculum maps, therefore, the teachers in the project generally resorted to the practice of assigning contracts in simple numerical sequence, booklet by booklet. Each student was able to proceed at his own pace, however; and as soon as he had completed one contract, another was given to him. Because this was true for every subject, each student always had a set of contracts upon which he was working. The effort that was subsequently made to develop a better contract assignment system will be described later in this book.

Testing and Scoring

All too often, teacher-made tests are unnecessarily cumbersome and, in this sense, wasteful of time. Because a program of individualized instruction requires highly specific instructional objectives and speedy assessment of student progress, it is of added importance to use tests that are easy to administer and score. This does not mean that compositional work is of little value. Far from it! The point is that the *format* of a test is not a trivial matter; a little care taken beforehand can save hours of correction time.

In the Franklin-Nettleton Project, a wide variety of testing devices was employed, from Rapid Raters (a punchboard device) to the traditional (and unwieldly) fill-in-the-blanks test. But we barely scratched the surface. A vast territory awaits exploration. The test game on pages 64-65 serves as an example of what can be done in this regard. Such a game board can be used with any number of two-choice test items; using twenty questions is especially convenient for the particular game board shown. Two advantages of this test game are that test results can be ascertained rapidly and that students enjoy working with it.

Earlier in this book, the importance of performance objectives (statements of criterion performance) was discussed. For the purpose of demonstrating the operation of the test game, your ability to recognize adequately formulated performance objectives will be challenged. Twenty objectives will be presented to you. Leaving aside the matter of content, decide whether each statement is expressed in terms of observable student performance. Using a penny, the point of a pencil, or your finger as a mover, take the beginning position in the black square on the left side of the game board. Here is the first objective:

1. Given a programmed booklet on Alaska, the student should, after carefully reading the booklet, be able to have a better understanding of the white man's influence upon the Eskimo culture.

Is this objective expressed in terms of observable student performance? If you think it is, move from the black square to the first empty circle *above* the square. If you think the objective is not expressed in terms of observable student performance, move to the first empty circle *below* the square. Go on to the second objective.

STUDENT..

TEST..

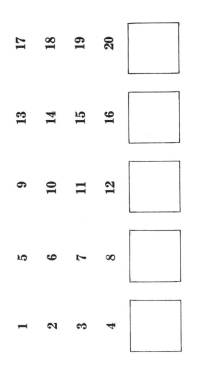

	A	B	C	D	E	F	G	H
A	Aoooo	Aooox	Aooxo	Aooxx	Aoxoo	Aoxox	Aoxxo	Aoxxx
B	Booox	Boooo	Booxx	Booxo	Boxox	Boxoo	Boxxx	Boxxo
C	Cooxo	Cooxx	Coooo	Cooox	Coxxo	Coxxx	Coxoo	Coxox
D	Dooxx	Dooxo	Dooox	Doooo	Doxxx	Doxxo	Doxxo	Doxoo
E	Eoxoo	Eoxoo	Eoxxo	Eoxxx	Eoooo	Eooox	Eooxo	Eooxx
F	Foxox	Foxoo	Foxxx	Foxxo	Foox	Foooo	Fooxx	Fooxo
G	Goxxo	Goxxx	Goxoo	Goxox	Gooxo	Gooxx	Goooo	Gooox

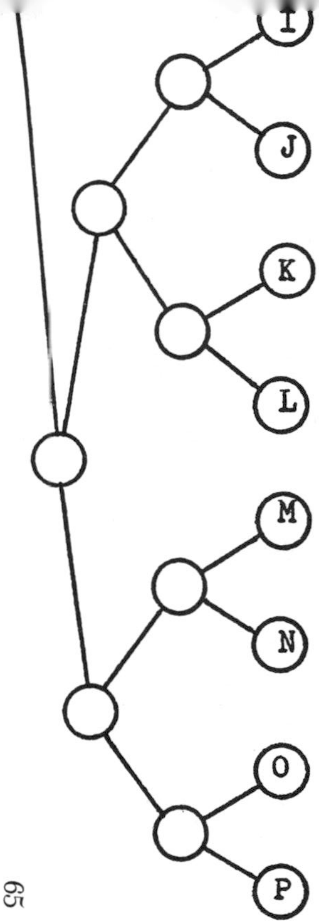

Top table (rows H–P; column headers not visible on this page):

Hoooo	Hooox	Hooxo	Hooxx	Hoxoo	Hoxox	Hoxxo	Hoxxx
Ixxxx	Ixxxo	Ixxox	Ixxoo	Ixoxx	Ixoxo	Ixoox	Ixooo
Jxxxo	Jxxxx	Jxxoo	Jxxox	Jxoxo	Jxoxx	Jxooo	Jxoox
Kxxox	Kxxoo	Kxxxx	Kxxxo	Kxoox	Kxooo	Kxoxx	Kxoxo
Lxxoo	Lxxox	Lxxxo	Lxxxx	Lxooo	Lxoox	Lxoxo	Lxoxx
Mxoxx	Mxoxo	Mxoox	Mxooo	Mxxxx	Mxxxo	Mxxox	Mxxoo
Nxoxo	Nxoxx	Nxooo	Nxoox	Nxxxo	Nxxxx	Nxxoo	Nxxox
Oxoox	Oxooo	Oxoxx	Oxoxo	Oxxox	Oxxoo	Oxxxx	Oxxxo
Pxooo	Pxoox	Pxoxo	Pxoxx	Pxxoo	Pxxox	Pxxxo	Pxxxx

Bottom table (rows A–P):

I	J	K	L	M	N	O	P
Axooo	Axoox	Axoxo	Axoxx	Axxoo	Axxox	Axxxo	Axxxx
Bxoox	Bxooo	Bxoxx	Bxoxo	Bxxox	Bxxoo	Bxxxx	Bxxxo
Cxoxo	Cxoxx	Cxooo	Cxoox	Cxxxo	Cxxxx	Cxxoo	Cxxox
Dxoxx	Dxoxo	Dxoox	Dxooo	Dxxxx	Dxxxo	Dxxox	Dxxoo
Exxoo	Exxox	Exxxo	Exxxx	Exooo	Exoox	Exoxo	Exoxx
Fxxox	Fxxoo	Fxxxx	Fxxxo	Fxoox	Fxooo	Fxoxx	Fxoxo
Gxxxo	Gxxxx	Gxxoo	Gxxox	Gxoxo	Gxoxx	Gxooo	Gxoox
Hxxxx	Hxxxo	Hxxox	Hxxoo	Hxoxx	Hxoxo	Hxoox	Hxooo
Ioooo	Iooox	Iooxo	Iooxx	Ioxoo	Ioxox	Ioxxo	Ioxxx
Jooox	Joooo	Jooxx	Jooxo	Joxox	Joxoo	Joxxx	Joxxo
Kooxo	Kooxx	Koooo	Kooox	Koxxo	Koxxx	Koxoo	Koxox
Looxx	Looxo	Looox	Loooo	Loxxx	Loxxo	Loxox	Loxoo
Moxoo	Moxox	Moxxo	Moxxx	Moooo	Mooox	Mooxo	Mooxx
Noxox	Noxoo	Noxxx	Noxxo	Nooox	Noooo	Nooxx	Nooxo
Ooxxo	Ooxxx	Ooxoo	Ooxox	Oooxo	Oooxx	Ooooo	Oooox
Poxxx	Poxxo	Poxox	Poxoo	Pooxx	Pooxo	Pooox	Poooo

Tree diagram with leaf labels: I, J, K, L, M, N, O, P

2. Given a string of beads that form a number and color pattern, the student should, by adding more colored beads to the string, be able to continue the pattern.

If you think this objective is expressed in terms of observable student performance, move to the next empty circle *above* the circle you are now on. If you think the objective is not expressed in terms of observable student performance, move to the next empty circle *below* the circle you are on. (Never retrace your steps; each new circle will always be slightly to the right of the one you leave.) Continue the procedure with the next two objectives.

3. Given a hypothetical need for a new law that will be initiated by a branch of government, and a randomly arranged list of steps that must be taken in order to create the law, the student should be able to list the necessary steps in correct sequence.
4. Given a set of tape-recorded piano tonal patterns based on combinations of the tonic triad and the major scale, and given the key signature of each pattern, the teacher candidate should be able to notate the patterns on the treble clef with 100 per cent accuracy in pitch and rhythm.

After responding to this fourth objective, your mover should be on one of the circles containing a letter. Write this letter in the first of the five answer boxes on the game board. Then return to the black square and decide on the next four objectives. After judging this set of four objectives, you must write a letter in the next answer box. Continue in this manner until you have responded to all twenty items and have a letter in each of the five answer boxes.

5. Given a magazine containing the needed illustrations, the student should be able to find at least ten pictures of people producing goods or services, label the pictures according to occupation, and state in writing what goods or services result from the work shown (90 per cent minimum accuracy required).
6. Given a list of activities carried on by the early settlers in North America, the student should be able to know what goods they produced, what productive resources they used, and what trading they did.

7. Given the statement, "Changing tastes of the American consumer changed the occupation required in our economy," the student should be able to comprehend the meaning of this statement.

8. Given the total amount of a loan, the monthly rate of interest, and the monthly payment rate, the student should be able to compute in writing the amount of principal repaid each month, the interest paid each month, the number of monthly payments necessary to repay the loan, and the effective annual interest rate.

Write your letter in the second answer box.

9. Given a list of 20 words, the student should be able to perceive that these words are arranged in alphabetical order according to the beginning letter of each word.

10. Given 20 statements, each purporting to reflect the thinking of Marshall McLuhan, the student should be able, with at least 90 per cent accuracy, to say which statements do represent McLuhan's views.

11. Given 20 dictated words containing the consonant elements "m," "p," "n," "t," "th," and "f," and the short vowels "a" and "i," the student should be able to hear, with at least 90 per cent accuracy, the designated consonant elements and short vowels in the dictated words.

12. Given the poem "The Sword," by William Blake, the student should be able to think of at least one way in which the symbolism in the poem could be interpreted.

Write your letter in the third answer box.

13. Given access to Heilbrenner's *The Worldly Philosophers*, the student should be able to have an intellectual grasp of the different points of view expressed in the book.

14. Given the terms "closed shop," "collective bargaining," "yellow-dog contract," and "interlocking directorate," the student should be able to develop an adequate understanding of each term.

15. Given a short story containing periods, question marks, exclamation points, quotation marks, and commas, the student should be able to have an awareness of the meaning of each kind of punctuation.

16. Given a set of three numerals that name whole numbers

not greater than six, the student should be able to list the four related addition and subtraction equations suggested by the numbers.

Write your letter in the fourth answer box.

17. Given the price of two different-sized packages of a product and the quantity of the product contained in each, and assuming equal quality, the student should be able to see how the unit price of each was determined.

18. Given an advertisement, the student should be able to comprehend: (a) how the advertisement catches the consumer's interest, (b) what information is given about the product, and (c) what information is given that is unrelated to the product.

19. Given the characteristics of a material for use as money, and the description of a situation in which silver became unavailable, the student should be able to understand how one or more other materials might be substituted.

20. Given the results of liver function tests performed on six jaundiced patients, the student should be able to list correctly at least five of the cases under the etiological headings of homolytic, hepatoullular, and obstructive jaundice.

Write your letter in the last answer box.

You should now have a letter in each of the five answer boxes. If so, you are ready to correct your test. To do this, you need to know what the five letters are supposed to be. In this case, they should spell the word "igloo." If your answers have not spelled this word, you have made one or more mistakes.

Suppose you had the letter "D" in your second answer box instead of the letter "G." The second answer box refers to test items 5, 6, 7, and 8. If you had the letter "D" there instead of the letter "G," you did not decide on this set of objectives correctly. What error, or errors, did you make? The answer key to the game you played makes up the bottom-right section of the game board. For the hypothetical situation involving the letters "D" and "G," you can use *either* the D column or the G column of the answer key. The results will be the same.

If you use the D column, simply go down that column until you come to the letter "G." The letter "G" in the D column is followed by two O's and two X's, and reads "Goxox." The O's refer to correct answers; the X's refer to incorrect answers. In this case that means you missed on the second and fourth items in the set of test items 5, 6, 7, and 8—in other words, test items 6 and 8.

If you use the G column, simply go down that column until you come to the letter "D." The letter "D" in the G column is followed by the same pattern of O's and X's as was the letter "G" in the D column; it reads "Doxox." Again, you are shown that you missed on the second and fourth test items in the set of test items 5, 6, 7, and 8—items 6 and 8.

Use the procedure described above to correct the test that you took.

To use the game board on pages 64-65 for *any* twenty-item, two-choice test you might construct for students, all you need do is arrange the pattern of correct answers so that the letters in the five answer boxes will spell out a nonsense syllable or word of your choice. The answer key section will be automatically adapted to your code syllable or word, and can be used to score any student's test.

Recording Student Progress

Acme Visible Record Books were used to help teachers maintain an accurate record of student accomplishment of performance objectives. A card (shown below) was inserted in each teacher's record book for each student in each subject. When a contract was assigned to a student, a diagonal line was drawn through the corresponding contract square in the grid. When the contract was completed, a second diagonal line was drawn through the square to form an X. The card shown below shows an assigned contract at Square 32, and a completed contract at Square 13. (Note: Each teacher used his own variation of this procedure.)

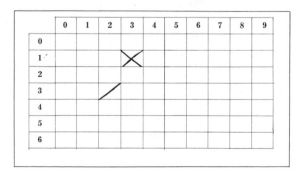

Successful Learning Activities

As might be expected, the things that did the best job of stimulating our project student were devices or situations that actively engaged them. Youngsters ordinarily do not want to be cast in the role of passive learners. Generally, the "lazy" student who "refuses to do anything" is protecting himself from failure. Doing nothing requires a determined act of will. In this sense, it is unpleasant work, preferable only as an alternative to further academic frustration and humiliation. Whenever the opportunity to engage in rewarding activity is available as a genuine option, most youngsters will respond positively.

Student-to-student Teaching

On a regularly scheduled basis, students from a senior high school individualized instruction project came to Franklin-Nettleton classrooms to help our students achieve their contract objectives. This turned out to be a beneficial arrangement for everyone concerned. The Franklin-Nettleton youngsters welcomed the additional attention; the high school students discovered that they, themselves, could learn by teaching; and the Franklin-Nettleton staff appreciated the assistance. Also, among the Franklin-Nettleton Project students, the abler pupils often helped the slower ones. We encouraged them to do so—and they found that they enjoyed it. Our conclusion was that student-to-student teaching is a powerful mode of instruction, and should be widely employed.

Programmed Instruction

The world of programmed instruction has been from the beginning almost completely surrounded by the paraphernalia of science. In view of its origins, this is hardly surprising, for it was initially explored by first-rate men of science who were investigating the implications of certain patterns of learning.

Science suggests technology. Many decent nonscientists will tell you that the two things are virtually synonymous. The first autoinstructional projects to emerge from the laboratories did little to dispel this notion. In one way or another, most of them involved the use of metal boxes, a fact that did not find favor within the world of liberal arts. People who are deeply committed to the humanities often seem to feel threatened by hardware, especially if it happens to be anything more sophisticated than the Model T. Programmed instruction—in the company of mechanical contrivances that flashed lighs, rang bells, and otherwise shamelessly comported themselves—was a perfect target for the dark arrows of Orwellian suspicion. And the arrows flew.

Another development did nothing to lessen anxiety among the nay-sayers. The audio-visual arm of the National Education Association came out in support of teaching machines and programmed instruction. Its big book on this subject became *the* major work in the field, and gave what may have been a decisive push for growth by this small-but-noisy new instructional methodology.

The legitimate interests of audio-visual experts being what they are, the emphasis was again on gadgetry. Awesome technological refinements occupied most of the newly-opened territory, and an ever-expanding empire was proclaimed. Small wonder that the cries of alarm grew louder in the ranks of the unanointed.

Unfortunately for their cause, the critics were ill-prepared to fight. But what professional humanists in disarray could not accomplish, a moderate faction *within* the advancing army could, and did.

Recovering from the gaudy thrill of being borne aloft by complicated machines, many of the faithful rediscovered the importance of programming. The value of designing and constructing ingenious presentation devices was admitted, but it was emphasized that machines were merely program holders. The content and ordering of instruction were what really mattered.

Events soon strengthened this point of view. Some equipment vendors had begun to make a brave show of independence. They marketed machines that needed only programs to become effective teaching devices. The remedy for this was simple enough, it appeared. All that any classroom teacher had to do was sit down and write his own programs. That was all. In the face of such a cheerful approach to the business of education, it is a pity to record that the facts of life obstinately refused to shape themselves accordingly.

When it finally became clear to hardware manufacturers that no amount of urging or friendly assurance would convince teachers that they ought to spend their time creating hearts for tin woodsmen, a collective rush started in the opposite direction. Programming, it was now agreed, should be left to the cool minds of psychologists and subject-matter experts.

A routine resembling a surgical operation was evolved. First, the body (of information) was brought in and strapped to the writing desk. Then it was put (or went) to sleep while its fate was discussed. The decision was always the same: stretch and fill. The specimen that emerged from the operation was noticeably changed. It was considerably bigger than before. Its speech was often slow, halting, and repetitive—a scholarly Tarzan equipped with a ready stock of unfinished "You, Jane; me, ____" statements for an academic society.

It would be a mistake, though, to suppose that this development was not worth while. It represented a significant improvement over the garrulous monologue of the ordinary textbook. The standards were high. A scientifically constructed program was expected to make a respectable showing in contests featuring matched groups of flesh-and-blood combatants. This was something new and revolutionary. The whole thing had a refreshing air of conviction about it.

The basic difficulty with programming may be one of perception. The need is to see how programming fits naturally into that vast web of communication whose strands run with perfect continuity between poetry and mathematics, science and art.

Many programmers seem to feel that art and science are naturally exclusive. You take your choice (the latter, if you can), but you cannot have it both ways. Therefore, programming should be regarded as an art form only insofar as it falls short of being scientific. According to this view, the scientist-programmer is exact, the artist-programmer imprecise.

The matter is not that simple. A programmer, we may say, is interested in predicting and controlling behavior. The prediction and control of events, human or otherwise, is the proper business of science. But is this not also a concern of the artist? To take an obvious example, any stage play worth the price of admission is written so that the audience will respond as the playwright intends. This is also true for a novel or a poem. It is what we mean when we say that an artist is in control of his material. He can make whatever he works with do what he wants it to do; and in every case this involves some kind of communication, even if upon occasion it is only with himself. It is in this sense that we need programmers who are artists, who understand with Sherwood Anderson that, "One works with words and one would like words that have a taste on the lips, that have a perfume to the nostrils, rattling words one can throw into a box and shake, making a sharp, jingling sound . . . ." We used programmed materials in the Franklin-Nettleton Project, but we found them to be uniformly dull and uninmaginative.

Other Instructional Resources

Rather than setting forth a comprehensive list of the instructional materials and equipment that we purchased, a few of the more notable items will be mentioned and some comments given on the over-all state of affairs as seen in retrospect.

Probably the single most valuable piece of equipment we acquired was the tape recorder. We had one for each teacher. A tape recorder is superior to a record player because it can be used to play teacher-prepared audio materials, the tape can be erased easily and re-recorded, and the stop and start buttons provide versatility. Junction boxes with several earphones connected were provided for every tape recorder to allow undisturbed listening. Each listening outlet had its own separate volume control—a small but important feature.

Using a small filmstrip projector with a small rear-projection screen was a particularly good instructional arrangement. The major limitation of this setup was the generally poor quality of the filmstrips available for viewing. It is surprising but true that filmstrips are almost uniformly dull in their treatment of subject matter. Why this should be so is difficult to understand. There are some programmed sequences in the medium, but these efforts have suffered from the same unimaginative approach that has characterized their printed counterparts.

The Bell & Howell Language Master, a machine for playing "talking cards," was another piece of equipment that was particularly useful. At least one other company—EFI with its Audio Flash Card—now offers a competing product; further entries in the field can be expected.

As major educational film companies offer more of their 16 mm. films in the more convenient form of 8 mm. film with *sound in cartridges,* the possibility of developing building-level holdings of 8 mm. sound films will have to be explored seriously. The use of federal monies in this sector of materials development seems appropriate.*

Student Effort

As with any other instructional arrangement imaginable, circumstances and human nature sometimes conspired to produce less than satisfactory habits of study in Franklin-Nettleton Project students. Whenever this occurred, an initial attempt was made to discover why the student in question had slackened his efforts. This was often difficult to determine. Frequently, therefore, a simple kind of negative motivation was employed. This consisted of placing the wayward student on a definite work schedule—so many minutes in the language arts room, so many in science, etc. In other words, the privilege of budgeting one's own time was temporarily taken from the student and he was put on a timetable that resembled that of a traditional school day. It is interesting to note that an arrangement designed to look like traditional schooling could prove to be such an effective punishment. More often than not, irresponsible students who were placed on this schedule soon began working to regain the freedom of self-scheduling. Of course, regimentation would not help students whose contracts were too difficult or, for some reason, irrelevant. There can be no substitute for appropriate learning.

Student Responsibility

Ability to take responsibility for learning varied enormously from student to student. Some were able to function more or less independently right from the start. Others were so used to work-

---

*Unfortunately, the use of federal funds at present is often too restrictive. One of the most glaring examples of this is the frequent requirement, even in the case of highly innovative projects whose development is contingent on intensive in-service programs, that all materials and equipment be itemized *before* the project in question begins. This puts the cart before the horse. It negates in advance many of the considered judgments that might be made in an effective in-service program, and is therefore wasteful of money.

ing only under the direct supervision of teachers that they found it hard to adjust to another way of doing things. Here again, the program tried to take student differences into account. Pupils who were ready to do so were given a large measure of responsibility for managing their affairs; those who initially experienced some difficulty in structuring their own learning schedule were provided with a greater amount of teacher direction.

Children cannot suddenly be turned loose to direct their own schooling. The matter is not that simple. What we need to do is provide a variety of learning activities that (1) will be highly motivating, (2) will have enough self-instructional features to ease the problem of classroom management, (3) can accommodate a wide range of individual differences, and (4) will encourage the accomplishment of worthy objectives.

Certainly, individualized instruction, when it is serious and not merely sincere, can help students move toward the ideal of self-directed learning. But this requires practice, learning by doing; and this means proceeding in stages, moving gradually from teacher-directed to self-directed activities. Preferably, this should begin early—when the child first enters school—and continue throughout the years of formal instruction. The trouble is not merely that it is hard for students to acquire the habits of independent study. Unfortunately, schools have not been organized to encourage students to function independently when, *individual by individual,* they become ready to do so. As for the proposition that such readiness itself can be taught, this has scarcely been explored in any significant way.

Student and Parent Reactions

Students and parents alike gave strong support to the Franklin-Nettleton Project. Attendance at P.T.A. meetings increased sharply, and for the first time in their lives many parents visited their child's school while it was actually in session. What helped to create this favorable attitude? As far as the parents were concerned, it seems reasonable to suppose that, although they might not understand the ins and outs of the program, they were very much aware of the sizable quantities of equipment and material that were being used to teach their offspring. Here was something tangible—visible products that transcended educators' jargon.

The students were also impressed by the machinery of instruction. Youngsters have an affinity for manipulative devices. It is not surprising that they tackled with enthusiasm the jobs of operating their own film projectors, filmstrip projectors, tape recorders, and record players. But it was more than the hardware of education that produced positive feelings on the part of students. When students were asked what they liked best about the project, the freedom to move around and see different teachers was mentioned over and over again.

In the spring of 1967, a simple attitude survey was conducted among project pupils and their parents. Parents were asked to respond to this statement:

I feel that my child's school experience this year is benefiting him/her (check one of the following)
more than_____
same as _____
less than_____ it did last year.

Of the 177 Nettleton parents surveyed, 101 responded. Of those responding, 74 per cent checked "more than," 19.8 per cent checked "same as," and 6.2 per cent checked "less than." Of the 67 Franklin parents surveyed, 49 responded, with 74 per cent checking "more than," 18 per cent checking "same as," and 8 per cent checking "less than."

The statement presented to project students read:

I have enjoyed school (check one of the following)
more than_____
same as_____
less than_____ I did last year.

Nettleton students returned 161 of the 177 forms given to them. The returns from Franklin students was 100 per cent of the 67 distributed. The Nettleton results were: "more than," 77 per cent; "same as," 13.7 per cent; and "less than," 9.3 per cent. The Franklin results were: "more than," 72 per cent; "same as," 12 per cent; and "less than," 15 per cent.

Spreading the Word

At one time or another, it seems educators have attributed virtually every kind of trouble in the schools to a failure in communication. We of the Duluth Public Schools have been no exception, and our interest in opening up better lines of communication has been a continuing one. Like other school systems, our concern has encompassed students, parents, and the public at large, but we have been concerned most particularly with the teaching staff and other personnel within the school system. We cannot claim to have been especially successful. Indeed, we have not as yet come up with anything more enterprising than a small monthly newsletter called *Inter-com*. Probably the most notable thing about *Inter-com* was the attempt to make it readable. The article on individualized instruction that follows appeared in November, 1966, in the form of an interview written by Herb Taylor, administrative assistant in charge of communications for the Duluth Public Schools.

The Devil's Advocate

. . . asks some pointed questions about individualized instruction

"Devil's Advocate" is the name given to an official whose duty it is to point out defects in the evidence when an individual is being considered for canonization by the Roman Catholic Church. Today it is also used to mean anyone who takes the negative side for the sake of argument—as *Inter-com's* reporter did in the following interview with Thorwald Esbensen, Assistant Superintendent for Instruction, and John Downs, Principal of Franklin-Nettleton, scene of a project in individualized instruction which is attracting wide attention both locally and nationally.

DEVIL'S ADVOCATE: Please be seated, Mr. Esbensen, Mr. Downs, I'm sure you both understand the purpose of this little interview?

ESBENSEN: No, not exactly.

D.A.: Well, you're certainly aware that various new instructional projects in Duluth are attracting national attention. They've attracted *our* attention, too. Anything that affects education affects *us*, and the Chief is very concerned.

ESBENSEN: May I ask why?

D.A.: Certainly. As everyone knows, idle hands are the Devil's workshop. If you succeed in improving the quality of the educational product, there will be fewer educational failures. That has negative implications for our work down here. When people are productively involved up there on Earth, *our* projects suffer. As the Chief always says: "There is more joy in hell over one dropout than over a whole multitude of skid row bums." You see, today's dropout is tomorrow's derelict. Our long-range goals are threatened by anything that improves educational quality.

ESBENSEN: Of course. That's what the Franklin-Nettleton Project is all about. Most of the youngsters in those two schools have been classified as "educationally deprived." We want to increase their chances of finishing school and becoming productive members of society.

D.A.: As I expected, Esbensen, you're a born troublemaker. We have a file on you, you know. Let me see . . . yes, here it is. "Eight years experience as classroom teacher; aroused opposition of principals with innovative techniques; first assignment was secondary social studies—wanted to throw out textbooks and marking system; following graduate work, headed English department in small school system, and *did* throw out textbooks . . . dangerous innovator and consistent advocate of individualized instruction." It's all here in black and white, Esbensen. Why can't you just leave well enough alone?

ESBENSEN: Because I don't think things are "well enough." You see, there's nothing new about the problems we face; educators have been aware of them for years. But now we have the possibility of new solutions. There's a new technology in education, new sources of funds . . .

D.A.: Technology? You mean all those gadgets, those "teaching machines"?

ESBENSEN: There's nothing really new about the "gadgets" either— except their availability. Forty years ago there was the Dalton Plan: a laboratory for each subject matter area, students budgeting their own time—but it didn't work because the teachers had to manufacture their own instructional materials. *Now* materials are available commercially . . .

D.A.: . . . Yes, and *now* you can squander money on elaborate hardware.

ESBENSEN: Not at all. Most of our efforts toward individualizing instruction revolve around printed materials. The hardware is highly visible, and it claims attention by comparison with traditional classrooms, but there's really not that much of it. Look at it this way. In a traditional classroom you buy 30 to 35 copies of a textbook, whereas in an individualized situation you buy five copies, because all students don't have to use it at the same time. This means you buy six or seven different texts for the same amount, and you get more bang for the buck.

D.A.: Don't kid me, Esbensen. You use workbooks that are *expendable*—the kids fill in the blanks and throw them away.

DOWNS: That's not true. The publisher may want us to operate that way, because he's interested in turnover. But we use plastic overlays which can be erased, or have the students write answers on a separate sheet. And as far as hardware is concerned, the elaborate devices are few and far between. We just make more use of the standard items. For example, we have a teacher to tape recorder ratio of one to one. And we use our 16 mm. projectors a lot—but do you know that most of them are over 15 years old and still operating satisfactorily? The *initial* outlay for the new technology may be greater, but after that, replacement costs are comparable to those in a traditional classroom.

D.A.: Ah, Mr. Downs—I'm not surprised that you're defending these new programs. After all, you were team leader of the original Duluth project—starting two years ago at Congdon Park—and your work there led to your new Principalship at Franklin-Nettleton. You're young, resilient, flexible . . .

DOWNS: I had five years of conventional experience before I started with Project Congdon, don't forget. I had to adjust, too—but the excitement and stimulation made up for the extra work. You see, I I had a chance to work creatively—to help develop the new approaches —and that's true of every teacher involved. At Congdon, Franklin and Nettleton, Ordean and Central—the participating teachers are all volunteers, and they all play a creative role in developing the projects.

D.A.: One minute, please. You now have about thirty teachers involved in these new programs, average age about 35. What about older teachers? What about the fact that you're asking for a personal and professional sacrifice? A teacher with many years experience is supposed to re-educate himself—with no incentive other than a pittance in terms of in-service training fees. He gets no advanced degree, no increase in salary-schedule status. He's not even a teacher anymore—he becomes what you call an "academic troubleshooter."

ESBENSEN: I object! We may be redefining the teacher's role somewhat, but he's still a teacher, with all the traditional duties and dignities of the profession. The same professional skills are demanded, but instead of working with a large group, all doing exactly the same thing, the teacher works with children in the specific areas where they most need help. And, the teacher gets a chance to specialize in his own areas of greatest strength. Instead of being an "educational broadcaster"—the sole purveyor of information in the classroom —he becomes an "educational decision-maker." He decides how the learning environment should be arranged, and what learning activities are most appropriate for any given student at any given time. He brings the student together with the appropriate materials, he becomes a conductor of learning, not a primary information source— but he's still a teacher—perhaps a more effective one than ever before. And as far as age is concerned, some of the most imaginative and lively teachers we have are those approaching retirement age. On the other hand, some people have hardening of the mental arteries at 25.

D.A.: But what about energy? Teachers are among the hardest-working of professionals. It's hard enough just to get through a day in the classroom. Now you're asking them to follow students around from room to room, to be continuously available for questions, to work long hours on new approaches and the preparation of student contracts . . .

Downs: One minute, please. You're forgetting that the teacher in the typical self-contained classroom is responsible for as many as nine areas of the curriculum. Multiply that by 30 students, and you've got 270 units of instructional responsibility. In the individualized program, the teacher has only one or two curriculum areas—and they are in the areas in which the teacher is most interested and best trained.

D.A.: Sounds like an assembly line to me. Any good teacher has a wide variety of interests; he's going to be stifled by teaching one subject all day long, year after year, even if it is his area of greatest interest. He's going to be buried in his own specialization.

Downs: You're exaggerating; things aren't nearly that cut-and-dried. The key concept in these new programs is flexibility, and that includes flexibility in interpreting the teacher's role.

Esbensen: We have no rules against a math teacher, for example, helping a good math student with whom he's developed a good relationship—helping him with his English, for example. The point is there are more opportunities for communication in an individualized program. The student—any student—has a better chance of being helped with any problem he can't handle.

D.A.: Okay, but what about the advantages of group activities, which you lose . . .

Esbensen: Please let me finish my point about communication. One of the real strengths of this program, according to the principals of the schools where we've tried it, is the opportunity it provides for the meaningful exchange of ideas among teachers. In the traditional setup, teachers are too isolated. They meet in the corridor or the lounge, but there's no ongoing exchange of ideas, no context for discussing problems and solutions. In an individualized program, it happens all the time—in fact, it's built right into the program.

D.A.: Fine—I'll concede that point. But please don't avoid my question about the advantages of group activity—advantages that you're losing with your new setup. Human beings have to learn to be effective in groups, because group activity is an absolute necessity in the adult world. Is it your goal to train only rugged individualists who know nothing about team work? That's one point, here's another: Some subjects—the humanities especially—deal with complex and sophisticated ideas. Self-directed study may be fine for the basic skills, but it's obvious that ideas and concepts need exposure and exposition by a trained adult—and *that* works best in the *large*-group situation. And at the same time, one would almost think from listening to you talk that there's *no* individualization in the typical classroom. Isn't it true that . . .

ESBENSEN: Of course! The vast majority of our teachers are doing outstanding work—real creative work—right in the self-contained classroom. Of course our teachers are trying to individualize the instructional process—our argument is that we can help them to do so by improving the instructional environment.

D.A.: Yes, and your improvements are pretty expensive. I won't bring up equipment again, but what about remodeling? Knocking down walls, adding electrical outlets . . .

DOWNS: Please take a closer look at Franklin. We have *not* remodeled that ancient building for the very reason that we want to prove that a completely individualized program can be organized in a *traditional* building.

D.A.: But what about the addition to the Chester Park School? You will be the first to admit that the entire design-concept is tailored to the needs of a program of the kind you've started at Franklin, Nettleton, and Congdon Park.

ESBENSEN: Indeed, yes. Chester is the first time we've gone "all the way," so to speak. The addition is designed with an individualized program in mind—and, if anything, it's *less* expensive than traditional construction! You see, there are fewer interior walls, and walls cost money. The twelve-room addition at Chester will serve as many students as a traditional structure: the difference is that there are *three* large areas of about 3600 sq. ft. each—instead of *twelve* areas of 900 sq. ft. The savings on unnecessary interior walls means the addition is actually cheaper to build. As I said, Chester Park goes all the way. Birchwood and Rockridge don't go quite as far—you see, we haven't rushed into anything. At the time Birchwood and Rockridge were being designed, we didn't feel we had enough experience to go all out for an individualized program. But the real point is, these two new schools *will* accommodate an individualized program very effectively. And, as we're proving at Franklin and Nettleton, any building in the system can be modified successfully with a minimum of remodeling.

D.A.: I think it's time to talk about guns and butter. The federal government has growing commitments abroad—what if federal grant programs are discontinued? *Then* what will happen to all these projects?

ESBENSEN: It's perfectly true that we've used federal funds to make these projects possible. The government money has helped us to make a beginning. But I think there's every reason to expect that the present commitment of the federal government in the field of education is going to be a growing one. The federal funds have given us a chance to prove something about education. If and when federal support is withdrawn, the public can judge whether or not the new approach has resulted in better education. If they decide that it has, we have also proved that it costs no more, in the long run, than do traditional approaches to building construction and classroom organization.

DOWNS: I hope we will all remember what the philosophy of education in a democracy really is: To give each child the best educational opportunity, as cheaply as possible—*not* just to give him the cheapest possible education.

D.A.: All right, you've brought up the subject of democracy, and I'm glad you did. I think your whole project is *anti*democratic. Your system allows the gifted student to move ahead and away from his peers, and the slower flounders without the stimulation and inspiration he'd get from working in a group with students more capable than himself.

DOWNS: That simply isn't true. In fact, the *opposite* is true. The teacher in the traditional classroom simply can't meet the special needs of either group—the gifted *or* the retarded. So, they are siphoned off and placed in special classes. But in a truly individualized program, there is the necessary flexibility to give specialized help when and wherever it's needed. For example, at Franklin-Nettleton we are taking the educable mentally retarded students who would ordinarily be separated into special classes, and putting them back with their own age peers. So far, it's working out well for all concerned, teachers and students alike.

D.A.: You both defend your projects very well—in fact it's rather obvious that if you can give evidence of success at the schools now involved you'd like to see this sort of thing expand to the whole school system. What will happen then? You're working with enthusiastic volunteers now. Do you hope to impose this new way of doing things on everyone in the system, whether they like it or not?

ESBENSEN: First of all, we have no intention of imposing anything on anybody. As new individualized projects are organized, we'll continue to seek *volunteers* to staff them. And while I'm at it, let me remind you that individualized instruction is not an "either/or" proposition. It doesn't happen only at special project schools—it's happening all the time in our self-contained classrooms, because every teacher realizes that self-guidance and self-direction are important educational goals for every pupil. Another thing: We didn't invent individualized instruction, and we didn't create the current trend in that direction.

Today's educational literature is full of it; it's the coming thing. We believe it's inevitable. But we *are* proud to be among the leaders in putting the ideas into action. And we're proud of the fact that the efforts here in Duluth are beginning to attract nationwide attention.

D.A.: All this is very exciting for the administrator—but what chance does the classroom teacher have to participate in this "inevitable trend"?

ESBENSEN: I think the best way to answer that one is to summarize just what an individualized program really is. Let me remind you of the one cardinal principle that undergirds all the others: An individualized program is one that makes it possible for each individual student to be engaged in those learning activities which are most appropriate for that student at any given time. Now, that's the one basic premise. Once you have stated that premise, and decided to operate from that premise—how it is worked out at each school will depend largely upon how the instructional staff in that school shapes it. In other words, if you were to look at the individualized projects at Congdon, Ordean, Central, Franklin, and Nettleton—you would see that there are different characteristics in each building. They are *not* all of a piece; there *are* marked differences—and the differences are due to the thinking of the staff people involved and the shaping of the instructional program by the staff. Individualized instruction is a concept that operates in two directions. We've been stressing individual opportunity for the student, but remember, it permits the teacher to be an individual, too. It gives the teacher his best chance thus far for individual creativity.

D.A.: Very well, gentlemen, I think that will be all. I have enough information to make a complete report to the Chief.

DOWNS: How do you think he'll react?

D.A.: Well, this isn't what he was hoping for. He would be pleased if I could report that the projects for individualized instruction in the Duluth Public Schools are impractical, ill-conceived and poorly implemented. Instead, I'll have to report that although the programs have not yet proved themselves, there's enough sound logic and real creativity behind them to indicate very good chances for success. He's going to be madder than blazes, and he has a very wicked temper.

ESBENSEN: What do you do in a case like that?

D.A.: Wait till he leaves his office, put the report on his desk, and make myself scarce. I wonder where in Hell I can hide this time.

1234

CHESTER PARK PROJECT

As "The Devil's Advocate" pointed out, the Chester Park Elementary School addition was our first attempt to design a building appropriate for individualized instruction. Essentially the structure is simply a shell containing three large classrooms and a library (or instructional materials center, as it hopefully will become). Each of these four areas is approximately the size of four ordinary classrooms. The absence of many of the interior walls normal to school buildings is an important feature of the building housing the Chester Park Project. The openness of the physical layout makes it easy for teachers to work together and for students to move about freely from one area to another.

Carpeting and acoustical treatment of ceilings reduce noise to a level below that generally found in traditional schools. The building currently houses 371 students (an overload of 11), 12 regular teachers, and a resource teacher who helps acquaint regular teachers with materials and procedures that might be used effectively with slow learners. A professional librarian is on hand two days a week. In co-operation with parent volunteers, he sees to it that the library is open for children at all times during the school day.

A large amount of in-service work preceded the debut of the Chester Park Project in the fall of 1967. The project staff was selected (again, on a voluntary basis) during the previous school year, and work with the staff got under way in January, 1967. Here the Research and Development Council of Northeast Minnesota (RAND Council), with its energetic executive secretary, Dr. Wesley Shepard, was of invaluable assistance. The RAND Council, despite money problems of its own, provided the financial support necessary to carry on an in-service program totaling about 200 hours and extending from January through August.

Staff Assignments

As in the case of the Franklin-Nettleton Project, teachers were assigned primary responsibility for certain subject matter areas— generally, two subject matter areas for each staff member. Three teams of four teachers each were organized, and each team was assigned to one of the intermediate grades. The project assignments were as follows:

Grade Four Team

Laurence Ruppel (Team Leader): science and physical education.
Patricia Ostrom: music and mathematics.
Donald Busch: language arts and humanities.
Patrick Dorin: social studies and art.

Grade Five Team

James Baird (Team Leader): science and art.
Karen Naslund: social studies and music.
Alicia Van Nevel: language arts and humanities.
Donald Roberts: mathematics and physical education.

Grade Six Team

Dale Koch (Team Leader): mathematics and music.
June Brieske: language arts and humanities.
Robert Cameron: science and art.
Thomas Ogston: social studies and physical education.

William C. Simmons was appointed to the principalship of Chester Park, and Karen Muller became the resource teacher. David Caucci, the librarian, rounded out the professional staff.

The Humanities

The emergence of the humanities as an integral part of the Chester Park Project's curriculum deserves special attention. Formal schooling has all too frequently been characterized by its division into separate subjects or courses taught in relative isolation. This fragmentation customarily produces students who possess a number of bits and pieces of learning, but have difficulty in perceiving connections among the various fields of human endeavor. The upshot of this state of affairs is cultural illiteracy, taken in its broadest sense; and there has been a corresponding need to reshape instructions so that it will become more relevant to the problems of daily living. At the secondary level, this need to see life whole is being met through the introduction of humanities courses. The Chester Park Project is an attempt to extend this effort into the elementary grades.

The central purpose of the humanities is to pose (not necessarily answer) man's most enduring question, "Who am I?" Such an undertaking requires that subject matter lines be crossed with impunity. In fact, it may be desirable to think of the entire curriculum as consisting of two major divisions: basic skills and humanities.

Certain subjects have customarily been taught as basic skills. Science, for example, has generally meant frogs and test tubes. Mathematics has been almost exclusively concerned with the manipulation of the language of numbers. This is all well and good, as far as it goes. But science and mathematics should also occupy outposts of influence within the humanities. The compelling ways in which science has affected society must receive fundamental attention; and mathematics, being the basis for automation, must accept partial responsibility for the coming redefinition of work and leisure in our society.

In this view of the humanities, all subjects have their part to play—and the time to begin is when the child first enters school. In Bruner's frequently quoted words: "It is possible to teach any subject to any child at any age in some form that is honest—and interesting. The challenge is to find how to represent the idea in a mode that is within the child's reach and then to proceed from there to a more precise and deeper representation."*

In-service Program

As usual, the major task of the in-service program was the writing of student contracts. In the case of the Chester Park Project, however, this work was complicated by the fact that none of the project teachers had any appreciable knowledge of the humanities. Consequently, the development of student contracts in the humanities was a formidable undertaking. We were fortunate in being able to acquire a humanities consultant to work with the entire project staff in an effort to upgrade their general background in this area.

Although we did not happen to do so, if our in-service learning assignments for teachers had been put into the six-point format of our student contracts, this is how they might have looked.

SAMPLE IN-SERVICE EDUCATION CONTRACT NUMBER 1

Content Classification

Philosophy of education.

Purpose

According to the February 21, 1967, issue of *Look*, "Marshall McLuhan is perhaps the most provocative and controversial thinker of this generation. His books, such as *Understanding Media*, have challenged many established notions about man and civilization." Formerly Director of the Center for Culture and Technology at the University of Toronto, Professor McLuhan now occupies the $100,000-a-year Albert Schweitzer Chair

---

*Jerome S. Bruner, "Liberal Education for All Youth," *The Science Teacher*, Vol.XXXII (Nov., 1965), p. 20.

in the Humanities at Fordham University in New York. The purpose of this objective is to acquaint teacher candidates with the views of this man, who says, "By the time this year's babies have become 1989's graduates (if college 'graduation' then exists), schooling as we now know it may be only a memory."

Criterion Performance

Given 20 statements, each purporting to reflect the thinking of Marshall McLuhan, the teacher will be able, with at least 90 per cent accuracy, to identify which statements do in fact represent McLuhan's views.

Sample Test Situation

Which of the following statements represent the thinking of Marshall McLuhan?
1. The medium is the message.
2. Television is hot.
3. Print is cool.
4. The key word in the new Electric Age is *involvement*.

Taxonomy Category

Comprehension.

Resources

Book: *Understanding Media*, by Marshall McLuhan.

Article: "The Future of Education: The class of 1989," by Marshall McLuhan and George B. Leonard, *Look*, February 21, 1967, page 23.

Article: "The Message of Marshall McLuhan," by Edwin Diamond, *Newsweek*, March 6, 1967, page 53.

Film: *Child of the Future* (National Film Board of Canada).

Book: *The Medium Is the Massage*, by Marshall McLuhan and Quentin Fiore.

Article: "From Instruction to Discovery," by Marshall McLuhan, *Media & Methods*, October, 1966, page 8.

Article: "What TV Is Really Doing to Your Children," by Marshall McLuhan, *Family Circle*, March, 1967, page 33.

Film: *The Medium Is the Massage* (McGraw-Hill Book Co.).

Article: "Marshall McLuhan Massages the Medium," by Marshall McLuhan, *Nation's Schools*, June, 1967, page 36.

Article: "A Schoolman's Guide to Marshall McLuhan," by John M. Culkin, *Saturday Review*, March 18, 1967.

Sample In-service Education Contract Number 2

Content Classification

Construction of student contracts in an in-service training situation.

Purpose

For many years, educators have talked about the importance of educational objectives. A well-written instructional objective should make clear to teachers, students, and other interested persons what it is that needs to be taught—or what it is that has been taught. Unfortunately, school systems generally do a very poor job of setting forth instructional objectives. For the most part, these aims of instruction consist of solemn pronouncements entombed in weighty, but largely useless, curriculum guides prepared by long-suffering committees of classroom teachers and supervisors. The purpose of this contract is to help teachers learn how to work out instructional objectives in terms of observable student behavior, for this is what will make it possible for them, as teachers, to tell how well they are doing whatever it is they are trying to do.

Criterion Performance

Given both a subject matter field and difficulty level of the teacher's choice, the teacher will be able to develop a set of instructional contracts according to the six-part format of content classification, purpose, criterion performance, sample test item or situation, taxonomy category, and resources.

Sample Test Situation

The teacher, either with or without in-service consultant help, and over a period of time designated by the teacher, will make his own determination of his achievement of the criterion performance set forth in this contract.

Taxonomy Category

Invention.

Resources

Preparing Instructional Objectives (Mager).
Working Out Instructional Objectives (Esbensen).
Taxonomy of Educational Objectives. Book I: Cognitive Domain (Bloom).

Education Index
In-service consultants.
Etc. (to be listed during in-service work).

As has been stated, we have had plenty of trouble putting together worthwhile student contracts in the humanities. So far, we have only begun to scratch the surface of what we would like to do. But a start has been made, and we are encouraged. On the pages that follow are some examples of what we are up to in the way of student humanities contracts.

67-1 Hu 6

Name _____

Date issued _____

Date due _____

Content Classification

Latin America.
    Pre-Columbian art.

Purpose

To engage students in an activity that will encourage creativity, provide some insight into pre-Columbian art, help students understand why and how a cultural past is preserved, and create an interest in architectural drawing.

Criterion Performance

Given ancient Latin American art pictures and modern architectural drawings, the student will be able to design an apartment building, house of worship, office building, or library in a modern style using pre-Columbian motifs.

Sample Test Situation

Open book.

Taxonomy Category

Invention.

Resources

Treasures of Ancient America (book).
The Art of Ancient America (book).
The Artistic Revolution in Mexico (filmstrip).
The Incas, the Mayas, and the Aztecs (filmstrip).

The Rainbow Book of Art (book).
Houses (book).
Big City Homes (book) and *All the Ways of Building* (book).
The First Book of Skyscrapers (book).
American Houses (book).
The Modern World (book).
Mexico (depth study, cross-media kit).
Exploring American Neighbors (book).
Leonardo Da Vinci (film) and *1492* (film).
House Beautiful, Better Homes and Gardens, and other magazines.
American Architecture in the 17th Century, Pt. 1 (slide set).
The Architecture of Thomas Jefferson (slide set).
Design (magazine).
Modern Architecture in Europe (slide set).
Modern Architecture: The University of Mexico (slide set).
The Land and People of Central America, by Ruth Karen (book).
The First Book of the Ancient Maya, by Barbara Beck (book).
Mexico, by Frances E. Wood (book).
Encyclopedia of Modern Architecture, by Wolfgang Pohnt (book).
Buildings for Industry, Volume II, by Walter Henn (book).
One Hundred Years of Architecture in America 1857-1957, by Frederick Butheim (book).
The Skyscraper (film).
Art of the Middle Ages (film).
Art: What Is It? Why Is It? (film).
Chartres Cathedral (film).
The City As Man's Home (film).

6HU-5

Name _____

Date issued _____

Date due _____

Content Classification

Comparison of cities.
  Brazil.

Purpose

To give the student an opportunity to compare life in several Brazilian cities.

Criterion Performance

Given a series of slides or photographs of Rio de Janeiro, Brazília, São Paulo, and Belém, the student is able to discuss and/or write how one would live there in terms of the following:

1. Which is the most modern?
2. Which is the newest?
3. Which city seems to be the most planned?
4. Which city has a world-famous carnival?
5. Which city is the closest to the equator?
6. In which city is poverty most evident?
7. What kinds of people do you see in each city?
8. In which city would you imagine having the most fun?
9. Are dark-skinned people usually poorer than light-skinned people? Are there any historical reasons for this?
10. Which city looks most like a city in the United States? Do you suppose that people there might also act more like us?

Sample Test Situation

See Criterion Performance.

Taxonomy Category

Invention.

Resources

Teacher-led presentation.
Tape-slide presentation #6Hu-B.
Gunther: *Inside South America* (book).
Tape #6Hu-D and study guide.
View filmstrip #1115, Rio de Janeiro and Brazília.
View filmstrips #1163 and 1164, Brazil.

Mu-Hu 201

Name _____

Date issued _____

Date due _____

Content Classification

Folk singing.
    Latin America.
Folk dance.
    Latin America.

Purpose

To develop an interest in and understanding of Latin American folk music and dance through active participation in singing and dancing.

Criterion Performance

Given a folk song of one of the Latin American countries and appropriate harmony and rhythm instruments, the student is able, with other students, to perform the song using English or Spanish lyrics and, where possible, accompany the song with instruments and dance.

Taxonomy Category

Application.

Resources

Rhythm and harmony instruments, such as bells, autoharp, ukulele, maracas, drums, etc.

"La Vidalita," p. 121, *Exploring Music, Book 6,* and accompanying recording (Uruguay and Argentina).

"Carmen, Carmela," p. 120, *Exploring Music, Book 6,* and accompanying recording (Mexico).

"Me gustan todas," p. 122, *Exploring Music, Book 6,* and accompanying recording (Spain, South America).

"Río, Río," pp. 124-125, *Exploring Music, Book 6,* and accompanying recording (Chile).

"In Bahía," pp. 126-127, *Exploring Music, Book 6,* and accompanying recording (Brazil).

"Water Come a Me Eye," pp. 128-129, *Exploring Music, Book 6,* and accompanying recording (Jamaica).

"Hosanna," pp. 130-131, *Exploring Music, Book 6,* and accompanying recording (Jamaica).

"¡Compren tamales!," p. 20, *Studying Music, Book 6* (Mexico).

"Mountain Climbers," p. 42, *Studying Music, Book 6,* and accompanying recording (Mexico).

"Rosita de Monterey," p. 53, *Studying Music, Book 6* (Mexico).

"Fiesta," p. 178, *Studying Music, Book 6,* and accompanying recording (Mexico).

"El loro," pp. 192-193, *Studying Music, Book 6* (Venezuela).

"Down by the River," p. 15, *Studying Music, Book 6* (West Indies).

"I Build Me a Little House," p. 56, *Studying Music, Book 6,* and accompanying recording (Jamaica).

Conciones De Honduras, a booklet of songs of Honduras, Pan American Union, 1960.

"La Cucaracha," p. 162, *Voices of the World* (Mexico).

"Cielito Lindo," p. 164, *Voices of the World* (Mexico).

"La Raspa," p. 165, *Voices of the World* (Mexico).

"Song to the Sun," p. 166, *Voices of the World* (Mayan chant).

"The Count of Cabra," p. 167, *Voices of the World* (Brazil).

"The Cat," p. 168, *Voices of the World* (Brazil).

"Sambalele," p. 189, *Voices of the World* (Brazil).

"River, River," p. 170, *Voices of the World* (Chile).

"The Tortilla Vendor," p. 171, *Voices of the World* (Chile).

"My White Horse," p. 172, *Voices of the World* (Chile).

"The Lonely Cowboy," p. 173, *Voices of the World* (Argentina).

"Trees," pp. 174-175, *Voices of the World* (Ecuador).

"Niño Chiquito," p. 176, *Voices of the World* (Venezuela).

"Poll Perica," p. 177, *Voices of the World* (Venezuela).

Educational Simulation

At the sixth grade level, a number of our student contracts are being tied to a year-long exercise in educational simulation called *Inter-nation Simulation.** This game is difficult to play; its complications are probably somewhat on the order of chess. However, its capacity to engage the energies and interests of participants seems beyond doubt, and the manner in which it appears able to reflect real-life situations is impressive.

For example, during the summer of 1967, as part of an in-service program for teachers, we spent a week playing *Inter-nation Simulation.* Because we were planning to use the game in the fall in connection with our Chester Park sixth grade study of Latin America, we used this same group of countries with the teachers. (One of the outstanding features of *Inter-nation Simulation* is its flexibility with regard to time and place. Because the basic structure of the game consists of a series of equations, it is possible to select any group of countries for any period of history. You pump the necessary data into the equations and begin from there. Instead of contemporary Latin America, for

*This highly complex instructional game was developed at Northwestern University and is now marketed by Science Research Associates.

instance, we might have selected Western Europe just prior to the outbreak of World War I.)

It wasn't until the second day of play that the game began to take hold; but when it did, emotions rose visibly. There was excitement in the air. The game started to mirror some facts of life. The Latin American press (news media are an integral part of the game) insisted on having its representatives attend meetings of the Council of Foreign Ministers. Initially, this prerogative of the journalists was resented by the diplomats. At one point, they voted to exclude all reporters from the council table, a decision which the press chose to ignore. However, by the end of the week, not only were reporters welcome at the council meetings, but almost every speech was for the benefit of the press; most genuine negotiating took place behind the scenes.

Another fact that the game forced the participants to recognize, in spite of themselves, was the indispensability of the United States in matters concerning the Western Hemisphere. Because the game was to focus on Latin America, no provision had been made for participation by the United States. By the middle of the week, however, it became obvious to everyone that trade with the United States was absolutely essential for the Latin American nations, and that the United States had to be dealt into the game in order to make it work under existing conditions.

We are hopeful that other facts of life will emerge for our students as they proceed to play *Inter-nation Simulation.*

Fourfold Use of Student Contracts

If we are to take seriously the goal of student direction, it behooves us to invent administrative procedures that will promote this development. One of our most significant advances in this direction, although we have barely begun to implement it, is the fourfold use of student contracts in the Chester Park Project. In earlier projects, student contracts (with a few notable exceptions) had been teacher-made and teacher-assigned. Under our current plan, each youngster, according to his own state of readiness, will be given the opportunity to work with student contracts according to four different approaches:

1. The teacher-made and teacher-assigned contract. This has been the standard approach in our individualized instruc-

tion projects. Under this arrangement, the teacher makes virtually all of the decisions concerning the content and sequence of learning activities.

2. The teacher-made but student-assigned contract. From the bank of contracts that the teacher has prepared, the student is able to select one of his own choosing. This option provides an interesting test of the belief that in matters of scope and sequence the teacher knows best. Earlier, in regard to our curriculum map efforts, we observed that instructional objectives do not appear to be as inexorably tied together as educators have often supposed. In any event, this contract approach can be expected to throw at least a little more light on this matter.

3. The student-made and student-assigned contract in an area identified by the student as one of his academic weaknesses. This means that each child will, in a preliminary way, be encouraged to assess some of his own instructional needs.

4. The student-made and student-assigned contract in an area identified by the student as one of special interest to himself. This is an "if I were king" or "if I had my druthers" sort of assignment. Inherent in it is the implication that we are not trying to produce a series of flat achievement profiles

Every youngster will be helped to use all four approaches in working with contracts. In each instance, however, the approach depends upon the pupil's own state of readiness. Taking responsibility for one's own learning is a skill that human beings must acquire gradually. We must begin with each child at the point where he is, and proceed from there.

Future Teachers

Working with students in a genuinely individualized fashion is a complex task calling for sophisticated, professional skills on the part of the entire staff. Needless to say, we have a long way to go. Adding to our problem is the fact that we sorely need a new product from college and university teacher education departments—the teacher for the decade ahead. Because teachers tend to teach in the way they have been taught, it is of crucial importance that institutions of higher learning begin a radical revamping of their teacher education programs—now, and without delay. This is no time for sprucing up a course here and there or altering an occasional requirement for graduation. What is wanted is a complete overhauling of the existing structure. As a starter, this might include: (1) the placing of teacher candidates in a completely individualized program of education, (2) the use of performance objectives as the basic ingredient of teacher education, and (3) making it possible for teacher candidates to begin working with children at the beginning of the candidate's career preparation, not toward the close of it. Other changes would also seem indicated, among them the abolishment of formal classes as such, and the creation of new kinds of learning spaces appropriate to the task at hand. In some instances, these physical changes have already occurred; indeed, physical changes appear to have developed substantially faster than educational methods.

But while the over-all teacher education picture looks dark, here and there an occasional spark of enlightenment sustains at least a flicker of hope. In Duluth, for example, the College of St. Scholastica has been developing an elementary teacher education program that may, in time, serve as an exciting model for others.

Project Criterion, the St. Scholastica program, has three main features: (1) the professional preparation of teachers is individualized, (2) performance objectives have been established as the measure of professional competency, and (3) teacher candidates have regular opportunities to work with children during the entire time of their professional preparation.

St. Scholastica's education courses are conducted through the use of printed instructional projects, or IP's, which are individual assignments to be completed by the teacher candidate at the candidate's own rate of learning. There are four kinds of IP's. First, there is the set of basic IP's that each teacher candidate must complete satisfactorily for an automatic grade of C. These IP's are printed on white paper and include not only projects for the teacher candidate to do by herself, but also projects for her to do with children. A second set of IP's is printed on green paper. These IP's allow the teacher candidate to explore a given field in greater depth. Satisfactory completion of a certain number of these IP's can mean raising the teacher candidate's grade to B. The third set of IP's, printed on gold paper, is made up of weighted IP's (WIP's), which are devoted solely to the teaching of children. Satisfactory completion of the child-oriented WIP's along with the development of voluntary IP's (VIP's, the fourth kind of IP's), which are undertaken by the teacher candidate with the approval of the appropriate college faculty member, may raise the candidate's final grade to A.

St. Scholastica's printed instructional projects and Chester Park's student contracts have the same format. An example of an IP for elementary teacher candidates at St. Scholastica follows:

Content Classification

Observing the world around us.

Purpose

The fact that the young child draws what he "knows," not what he sees, has some implications for the classroom teacher of art. One implication is that art instruction, among other things, should change a child's way of "knowing." This instructional project will give the teacher candidate a chance to try to bring about this kind of change in children.

Criterion Performance

Given a class of 2nd, 3rd, or 4th grade children, the teacher candidate will get from *each* child a *before* and *after* drawing or painting that will demonstrate the change brought about by the child's close observation and the new awareness as it has been guided and encouraged by the teacher candidate.

Sample Test Situation

The teacher candidate will hand in a *before* and *after* picture from *each* child to show a development in each child's ability to see accurately, as opposed to his former way of "drawing what he knows."

Taxonomy

Application.

Resources

Teacher-led presentation.
School Arts, November, 1963, pp. 19-20.
School Arts, December, 1965, p. 13.
School Arts, September, 1964, pp. 31-32.
School Arts, October, 1964, p. 22.
Education Index.

A Student's Day at School

Margo Fluegel, a sixth grade student at Chester Park Elementary School, lives eight blocks from school. She arrives by bus each morning at approximately 8 o'clock.

Upon entering the building, Margo goes directly to the cloak area to put away her outdoor clothing.

At 8:10, Margo checks herself in on the attendance board located in the sixth grade instructional area. This is a large, open space the size of four ordinary classrooms; carpeting increases the available working space. Here a hundred and twenty-some students and four teachers will spend the major portion of the day.

School does not officially begin until 8:30, so Margo and two of her friends look at some magazines in the library. No walls separate the library from the general instructional areas, which are immediately adjacent. Mobile shelves are the only visual barriers.

The school day begins in each homeroom with the Pledge of Allegiance and the National Anthem.

The thirty-minute homeroom period continues with a discussion of current events. Margo locates the Mediterranean Sea on a globe for her homeroom teacher, Robert Cameron.

Toward the close of the homeroom period, Margo plans her work schedule for the day. Each student is required to make out a daily schedule as a guide for his own activities, and he must budget his time around whatever formally structured group work the teachers may have scheduled. Although the exact individual study times planned by the student do not need to be rigidly adhered to, they should represent genuine approximations by the student.

At 9 o'clock, the homeroom period comes to an end and Margo begins her individualized academic work by taking a taped spelling test. This completes some work that was begun the day before, and is a relatively brief affair, consuming only about ten minutes in all.

Margo and Mrs. June Brieske discuss a new contract in language arts. At this time there is a consideration of any question the student may have regarding the intent of the contract. Each assignment carries a "due date" that is finally established by the teacher on the basis of what is known about a student's ability and work load, the difficulty of the contract, and other circumstances that may be relevant.

Margo locates some instructional materials to use in working on her new language arts contract. Whenever she feels ready to take the test that will measure her accomplishment of the objective designated by her contract, she may do so. She does not have to spend more time than she actually needs on any set of learning activities. The criterion is demonstrated achievement rather than time served.

Margo settles down for some concentrated work on her language arts contract. Should she experience any difficulty with the resources she is using, three courses of action are open to her. She may ask her teacher for direct help, . . .

She may receive assistance from a classmate, . . .

Or she may put aside her language arts work until later in the day when she can attend a teacher-led discussion for students who are working on the same contract or related contracts.

At 10 o'clock, Margo goes to her physical education class. Today it is ice-skating.

After her physical education class, Margo joins a group she has been working with on a science project —sending aloft a hot-air balloon.

At 11 o'clock, Margo returns to the sixth grade instructional area. Enroute, she stops briefly to watch a woodcut taking shape.

In the science area, Margo and three other students review with Mr. Cameron the results of the hot-air balloon project. From here ...

Margo joins a film group that has been working with another teacher, Thomas Ogston, on the editing of a student-made film. Modern schooling has a responsibility to help students become fully acquainted with nonprint media.

Just before lunch, Margo has a short session with her mathematics teacher, Dale Koch, on the topic of probability. Manipulative materials are useful in the formation of concepts.

Then it's time to eat. Some of the students, Margo among them, bring their lunch to school.

After lunch, Margo returns to the sixth grade instructional area, where her social studies teacher, Mr. Ogston, helps her get started with some work on map and globe skills.

A little later, a supervisor of student teachers who is visiting the individualized instruction project asks Margo some questions about it. The Duluth projects have had many visitors from different parts of this country and from abroad.

Latin America is the focus of the social studies program, and the entire sixth grade is involved in a year-long exercise called *Internation Simulation.* At 1:20, Margo meets with the Chilean Simulation Team. As reporter for this team, she takes notes for the next edition of the newspaper, *La Prensa de las Nacional.*

In connection with the simulation exercise, Margo consults David Caucci, the librarian. (Parent volunteers and students also help to keep the library functioning.)

At 1:45, Margo becomes a participant in a musical skills development group. Mr. Koch is the teacher. Following this, . . .

Margo's music contract calls for some independent study using a tape recorder and a filmstrip projector. The earphones make listening a private affair.

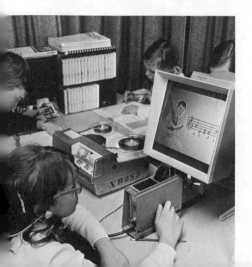

Rounding out the school day, Margo does a line drawing for an art contract. The time is 2:25.

At 2:45, school is dismissed. Margo may take some of her contract work home if she wishes, but homework is not mandatory. Motivation, not external pressure, is the ultimate key to student progress.

A Teacher's Day at School

Dale Koch, a mathematics and music teacher and leader of the sixth grade team at Chester Park Elementary School, arrives for work at about 7:15 A.M. He spends his preschool time preparing materials and planning future activities for the individualized program. Today he begins by making an introductory tape for a mathematics contract on the topic of probability.

A film previewing session follows. It may result in the addition of another instructional resource for a music contract on the piano.

At approximately 8 o'clock, Mr. Koch sits down with student teacher Clarence Grimsrud to discuss some student record information that will be used during the course of the day's work.

An annual event, the Youth Concert, is the subject of a conversation between Mr. Koch and the principal of Chester Park School, William C. Simmons. Students will attend the concert at Duluth's Arena-Auditorium, and plans must be made accordingly.

Custodian Gail Freeman gives Mr. Koch some last-minute help hanging a map that will be used during the morning's homeroom session.

School officially begins at 8:30. Following the Pledge of Allegiance and the National Anthem, Mr. Koch makes a general announcement to all four homerooms in the sixth grade instructional area.

The homeroom period usually includes a brief review of current events. During this half hour, students are also expected to "firm up" their study schedules for the day.

At 9 o'clock, Mr. Koch gathers together a small group of students for a presentation on the technique of graphing equations. Each of the five youngsters is working on a contract related to this problem.

When he has finished his work with the mathematics group, Mr. Koch moves among the students throughout his area, helping individual pupils with their independent learning activities. Here a boy receives assistance in working out the melodic line of a contract-assigned song.

An oral explanation sometimes accompanies the issuing of a new contract, most frequently when a new concept is being introduced. Students are encouraged to progress as rapidly as their individual capabilities will permit.

This young lady wishes to show her classmates some slides of Italy. This kind of student initiative is reinforced by the project's staff. Here Mr. Koch's colleagues, Mrs. June Brieske and Thomas Ogston, help to schedule the desired showing.

The field of educational simulation holds great promise for fostering skills in the area of group process and for cutting across traditional subject matter boundaries. With Mr. Koch's help, the music of the Brazilian composer Villa-Lobos becomes the center of attention for an *Inter-nation Simulation* team.

A 10 o'clock coffee break provides an occasion for conversation with staff members from the fourth and fifth grade levels of the project. Frequent interaction among all teachers in the project contributes to the strength of the over-all operation.

At 10:15, choir practice is held in the cafeteria. The youngsters are singing the round "Come Follow Me."

Back in the sixth grade instructional area, Mr. Koch gives assistance to individual students who need it. This discussion concerns a special problem in fractions.

At 11 o'clock, Mr. Koch teams up with fellow teacher Robert Cameron on a combined art and mathematics contract involving the construction of a tetrahedron model, to be followed by an art project using a tetrahedron design.

At the conclusion of his tetrahedron presentation, Mr. Koch makes a telephone call to the central office of the school district regarding some manipulative mathematics materials for the project.

Co-operation in analyzing student learning problems is an important characteristic of the project. Here resource teacher Karen Muller, Mr. Koch, and Mrs. Brieske (language arts) discuss what should be done about a student's reading difficulties.

Students enjoy using a calculator to solve mathematical problems. In this instance, Mr. Koch shows a student how to make some computations in connection with the *International Simulation* exercise.

A group discussion concerning the construction of a sphere for a humanities contract is next. The idea is to fashion a model of the earth and mark on it some patterns of distribution (language, food, etc.).

Just before lunch, Mr. Koch administers a test in mathematics. Every contract has a test or criterion task to measure a student's accomplishment of the designated instructional objective.

After lunch, school secretary Darlene Kranz helps Mr. Koch requisition supplies.

At 1:25, Mr. Koch talks with librarian David Caucci about the possibility of acquiring certain resource materials for a humanities contract in preparation.

Then it's time for another music group.

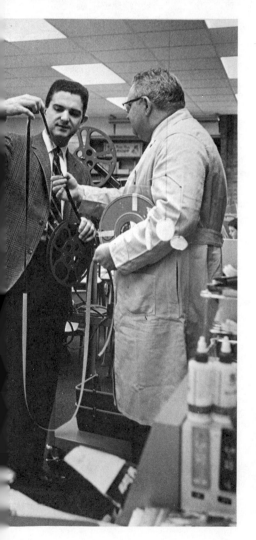

Later in the afternoon, Mr. Koch goes to the fifth grade area to invite the co-ordinated use of some mutually-shared materials. There, three fifth grade girls have posed a question regarding the painting of a puppet theater they are making.

Mr. Koch and James Baird, leader of the fifth grade team, agree on the scheduling of a film that both grade levels wish to use — for different purposes.

Finally, it's dismissal time.

But Mr. Koch's duties are not at an end. A parent-teacher conference has been set for 3 o'clock. During such meetings can occur the most valuable kind of reporting that home and school have to offer each other.

Before the day is done, a team meeting is held, including regular teachers and student teachers. Larger, all-project staff meetings are also conducted as needed.

At 4:30, Dale Koch and social studies teacher Thomas Ogston leave school. Both men are taking home equipment and materials that they will use during the evening hours as they prepare for the next day's work.

In Conclusion

It is difficult to state with assurance that individualized instruction is indisputably superior to traditional forms of schooling. As measured by a traditional kind of standardized achievement test (the Iowa Tests of Basic Skills), the results show a general standoff in performance. Moreover, we have been unable to find suitable tests in such important areas as creativity, improvement in study habits, growth in acceptance of responsibility, and the like.

There are, however, possibly useful indicators at hand. Although we have scarcely made a beginning in this regard, some promising points of exploration may be suggested. When a school principal reports a drop in absenteeism among project students, this may tell us something about student attitudes toward school. When a district survey reveals that while school window breakage in the district as a whole *increased,* window breakage for project schools in the inner-city core substantially *decreased,* this fact may tell us something about student attitudes toward school.* Of course, evidence of this kind needs to be accumulated over a number of years. We are certainly not claiming anything definite at this juncture.

Reports from our students, from our teachers, and from the parents of our students also give us clues. The mother of one of our mentally retarded pupils informed us that until her daughter joined the project, the child was taking medication for a serious bed-wetting problem. It was believed that the bed-wetting was in some way related to the girl's expressed anxiety about her work in school. After several weeks in an individualized instructional program, the bed-wetting stopped, the medication was discontinued, and the child showed for the first time an active interest in going to school. A sixth grade boy, an extremely shy and withdrawn student when he first enrolled in the individualized program, is now chairman of a class oceanography project and consultant to an aerospace project that plans to launch four multistage rockets during the current school year.

* For the district as a whole, glass replacement rose from 1,263 panes during fiscal year 1965-66 to 1,530 during fiscal year 1966-67. During the same period, glass replacement at the Franklin and Nettleton schools decreased from 174 panes to 95.

Comments from Students

STUDENT A: "I didn't like school before, but I like it now."

STUDENT B: "I like the way we can choose what materials we want."

STUDENT C: "In this type of school a person can learn things faster and enjoy school at the same time."

STUDENT D: "There isn't anything I don't like about this program, and I think I'd get awful bored in a different school."

STUDENT E: "My parents don't have to *make* me go to school anymore."

STUDENT F: "I like the free movement. I like the way we can work at different speeds and grade levels."

STUDENT G: "It would be hard to go back to the old way."

STUDENT H: "I think this school is the best in the whole world."

Comments from Parents

PARENT A: "How does it feel to be ten feet tall? It is the first time in three years that my son has liked school. This program has done so much for him."

PARENT B: "(My child) likes to choose his own study materials."

PARENT C: "(My daughter) doesn't get bored waiting for the rest of the class to catch up with her."

PARENT D: "(My son) never feels pressured to keep up with any other child. This makes him not so nervous."

PARENT E: "(My girl) works more happily when she can choose the subject she is going to study."

PARENT F: "(My boy) enjoys being able to work with a variety of teachers, and I think he is learning to get along better with different personalities. It'll help him in junior high."

PARENT G: "I am very happy that some school is finally going to help (my son) learn how to use his time well."

PARENT H: "(My daughter) has never been able to work on her own. She is learning how to study in this school."

PARENT I: "(My youngsters) used to be nervous and tense, but aren't now."

PARENT J: "My child enjoys this school."

PARENT K: "Our children don't want to move away from this school."

PARENT L: "John is no longer afraid of his teacher, nor is he shy."

PARENT M: "Our children like the freedom."

PARENT N: "My daughter understands the teachers better."

PARENT O: "If Joe doesn't like one teacher, he can go to another."

PARENT P: "I appreciate the special consideration given Jane. I never got treatment like this."

PARENT Q: "You must work extra hard to treat everyone as individuals."

PARENT R: "This is the first time in my life that one of my children has had to be restrained because of wanting to go to school too early. The only reason for that is that her school life is a happy and educational one."

Summing Up

Understandably, this program has neither pleased all parents nor motivated all students, and the distance between where we are and where we would like to be is vast indeed. Nevertheless, we are emboldened to predict that, despite the many vicissitudes of its practitioners, individualized instruction is here to stay. But this will be true only to the extent that it is viewed as an intelligent quest, an imaginative search for better ideas with which to improve the process of education and not as a blueprint or as a product.

In *The Miracle Ahead,* pollster George Gallup summarizes the task before us:

In any discussion of education it must be borne in mind that we are only now beginning to be dimly aware of the great potential of the human mind, and we have scarcely reached the point of recognizing that mankind must face up to the Herculean task of how best to develop the great and largely unused powers of the brain, and how best to apply these powers for the good of mankind once they are fully developed. To ignore the revelations of recent years would be unthinkable; and to fail to take advantage of them in designing an educational program for the future, unpardonable.*

*George Gallup, *The Miracle Ahead,* New York: Harper & Row, Publishers, 1964, p. 30.

Selected References

ARCHAMBAULT, REGINALD D. (ed.). *John Dewey on Education, Selected Writings.* New York: Modern Library, Inc., 1964.

ASHTON-WARNER, SYLVIA. *Teacher.* New York: Simon and Schuster, Inc., 1963.

BLOOM, BENJAMIN S. (ed.). *Taxonomy of Educational Objectives. Handbook I: Cognitive Domain.* New York: David McKay, Inc., 1956.

BRUNER, JEROME S. *Toward a Theory of Instruction.* Cambridge, Mass.: Harvard Univ. Press, 1966.

BUGELSKI, B. R. *The Psychology of Learning Applied to Teaching.* Indianapolis, Ind.: The Bobbs-Merrill Co., Inc., 1964.

CORRIGAN, ROBERT E., and ROGER A. KAUFFMAN. *Why System Engineering.* Belmont, Calif.: Fearon Publishers, 1965.

CRAM, DAVID. *Explaining "Teaching Machines" and Programming.* Belmont, Calif.: Fearon Publishers, 1961.

GALLUP, GEORGE. *The Miracle Ahead.* New York, Harper & Row, Publishers, 1964.

MCLUHAN, MARSHALL, and QUENTIN FIORE. *The Medium Is the Massage: An Inventory of Effects.* New York: Bantam Books, Inc. 1967.

MAGER, ROBERT F. *Preparing Instructional Objectives.* Belmont, Calif.: Fearon Publishers, 1962.

MAGER, ROBERT F., and KENNETH M. BEACH. *Developing Vocational Instruction.* Belmont, Calif.: Fearon Publishers, 1967.

POTTER, DAVID, and MARTIN P. ANDERSON. *Discussion: A Guide to Effective Practice.* Belmont, Calif.: Wadsworth Publishing Co., Inc., 1963.

SANDERS, NORRIS M. *Classroom Questions—What Kinds.* New York: Harper & Row, Publishers, 1966.

SYMONDS, PERCIVAL M. *What Education Has To Learn from Psychology.* (3rd ed.). New York: Teachers College Press, 1965.

TAYLOR, RALPH W. *Basic Principles of Curriculum and Instruction: Syllabus for Education 305.* Chicago: Univ. of Chicago Press, 1950.